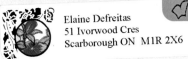

CUBA

SERGIO GUERRA VILABOY holds a Ph.D. in philosophy from the University of Leipzig. He is head of the History Department at the University of Havana and is executive secretary of the Association of Latin America and Caribbean Historians. He is also on the editorial boards of several magazines, including *Tzintzun* and *Ulúa* (Mexico), *Investigación y Desarrollo* (Colombia*), Kó-Eyú Latinoamericano* (Venezuela) and *Contexto Latinoamericano* (published by Ocean Sur); he has given talks at a number of universities; and has written several books, including *Paraguay: de la independencia a la dominación imperialista* (1991), *Los artesanos en la revolución latinoamericana* (2000), *El dilema de la independencia* (2000), *Cinco siglos de historiografía latinoamericana* (2003), *Historia de la Revolución Cubana* (2005), *Breve historia de América Latina* (2006) and *Ernesto Che Guevara* (2007).

OSCAR LOYOLA VEGA holds a Ph.D. in history and was deputy dean of the School of Philosophy and History at the University of Havana between 1993 and 1997 and presided over its Doctoral Commission. He has given talks at universities in a number of countries and co-authored several books, including *La Guerra de los Diez Años* (1989), *Cuba y su historia* (1999) and *Historia de Cuba 1492-1898. Formación y liberación de la nación* (2001).

CUBA
A HISTORY

Sergio Guerra Vilaboy
Oscar Loyola Vega

Ocean Press
Melbourne ■ New York
www.oceanbooks.com.au

ISBN 978-0-9804292-4-4
Library of Congress Catalog Card Number 2010920611
First edition 2010
Printed in Mexico by Worldcolor Querétaro, S.A. de C.V.

PUBLISHED BY OCEAN PRESS
Australia: PO Box 1015, North Melbourne,
              Victoria 3051, Australia
USA: 511 Avenue of the Americas, #96
              New York, NY 10011-8436, USA
E-mail: info@oceanbooks.com.au

OCEAN PRESS TRADE DISTRIBUTORS
United States and Canada: Consortium Book Sales and Distribution
              Tel: 1-800-283-3572 www.cbsd.com
Australia and New Zealand: Palgrave Macmillan
              E-mail: customer.service@macmillan.com.au
UK and Europe: Turnaround Publisher Services
              E-mail: orders@turnaround-uk.com
Mexico and Latin America: Ocean Sur
              E-mail: info@oceansur.com

Ocean Press
Melbourne ■ New York
www.oceanbooks.com.au

www.oceanbooks.com.au
info@oceanbooks.com.au

Contents

1
From the Original Inhabitants to Slave Plantations

"The fairest island human eyes have yet beheld... It is certain that where there is such marvellous scenery, there must be much more from which profit can be made."

—Christopher Columbus, October 24, 1492

The Cuban Archipelago
and the Indigenous Population

Christopher Columbus reached the northern coast of eastern Cuba on October 27, 1492. The Cuban archipelago, consisting of one large island, several smaller ones and hundreds of islets, amazed the Spaniards. They found Cuba a very pleasant sight, with its great variety of flora, beautiful scenery, delightful climate and low mountains, Turquino Peak being the highest at 6,476 feet (1,974 meters) and gentle rivers, like the Cauto, which flows for 213 miles (343 kilometers).

Indian peoples had apparently lived in Cuba for around 10,000 years, the first groups arriving from the Mississippi and Florida regions by way of Grand Bahama Island. Later waves of Arawaks arrived from what is now Venezuela and Central America, island-hopping along the Antilles. These migrations were still occurring in 1492.

The indigenous peoples of Cuba—the Guanahatebeys, Siboneys and Tainos—were generally hunters, gatherers, fishermen and early farmers. These groups of Indians never attained the cultural complexity and development of other societies in South and Central America, but some developed rudimentary agriculture and pottery. They grew tobacco, corn and yucca and lived in small hamlets either inland or on the banks of rivers.

By the time the Spaniards appeared on the scene, some of these societies had already achieved greater complexity, reflected in the custom of burying their dead and the emergence of a social division of labor, distinguishing between the tribal chief, the religious leader and the rest of the community. They also played sports, called batos, engaged in ceremonial songs and dances, and portrayed their surroundings in pictographs. The Spaniards' arrival halted the development of these indigenous societies in Cuba and almost entirely wiped them out.

Conquest and Colonization

Under the Santa Fe Pact signed by Christopher Columbus and the Catholic Monarchs, Isabella and Ferdinand, Columbus was to sail around the earth to reach Cipango and Cathay, in Asia. The pact stated how much of the booty obtained on the voyage would go to the contracting parties and how much the sailors would receive.

Cuba had almost none of the gold and silver the Spaniards sought for their nascent capitalist economy in Europe, so Columbus prioritized the colonization of Hispaniola to the east (the Dominican Republic today). On his second voyage, in 1493, he skirted the southern coast of Cuba, putting ashore near Cape San Antonio in the western part of the island, and he forced his crew to sign a document stating they had reached the mainland. He then returned to Hispaniola, which he viewed as more important; for the next 15 years, the Spanish monarchy displayed very little interest in Cuba.

In 1508, Nicolás de Ovando, governor of Hispaniola, was instructed to organize an expedition to circumnavigate Cuba. Sebastián de Ocampo carried out this order and proved it was an island. A conflict developed between the Castilian monarchs and Columbus's son, Diego Bartolomé Columbus, the new governor of Hispaniola. So it was Diego Velázquez, rather than Diego Bartolomé Columbus, who was appointed governor of Cuba in 1510 and he was ordered to begin the conquest and colonization of the island.

Velázquez arrived in Cuba near what is now Maisí and faced little resistance from the indigenous population. He founded Nuestra Señora de la Asunción de Baracoa, the first Spanish settlement in Cuba, at the end of 1510 and the beginning of 1511. The Spaniards soon expanded throughout the island: a brig went along the northern coast; a column of men under the command of Francisco de Morales—who was soon replaced by Pánfilo de Narváez, a close friend of Velázquez's—advanced through the central part of the island; and Velázquez himself traveled along the southern coast. None of the indigenous people put up much resistance, except for Hatuey, an Indian chief from Hispaniola, who was burned at the stake. So the conquest was quickly achieved.

Six new settlements were founded between 1512 and 1515 at San Salvador del Bayamo, Santísima Trinidad, San Cristóbal de La Habana, Sancti Spíritus, Santa María del Puerto del Príncipe and Santiago de Cuba (which replaced Baracoa as the seat of the island's government). Some of these settlements were later moved to their present locations.

The Spanish idea of developing a colony by encouraging the emigration of families laid the basis for future conflicts between the representatives of the monarchy and the top level of local government, the town councils, whose members elected their own mayors. Over the decades, the town councils became ever more exclusive oligarchies reflecting the interests of particular regions and these frequently clashed with the interests of the mother country. Apart from the governor of the island, the most important Spanish officials in Cuba were the inspector (or agent), the accountant and the treasurer. The town councils also sent representatives to the Cortes. The Catholic Church also had a strong presence, whose main duty was to proselytize among the Indians.

One of the conquistadors' main goals—finding gold—was not achieved in Cuba, which had no large deposits of that mineral. Some gold was obtained by forcing Indians to pan the rivers; but by 1542, raising cattle, pigs and horses—both for local consumption and for export to the newly conquered territories in South America—was becoming the basis of the new economy. Cattle ranching did very well in the forested areas of the island. At the same time, the need to survive forced the Europeans to use plants cultivated by the indigenous peoples, such as yucca, from which a substitute for bread was made. Tobacco was another plant the Spaniards learned about from the Indians and gradually it became very important to Cuba's economy.

Without authorization, Velázquez allocated Indian land to his men. In 1536, following the established practice, the town council of Sancti Spíritus issued land grants to Spanish soldiers. This did not imply legal ownership as the land officially belonged to the king of Spain. Rather, it meant the right to use it on payment of a fee to the Spanish monarchy and the Catholic Church. The land grants were made in the form of farms of various sizes. The contradiction between right to use the land and lack of legal title would, in the long run, create a serious impediment to the development of capitalism in Cuba.

An indigenous work force was distributed along with the land, tying the Indians to the Spaniards not in the classical form of slavery but in a bond similar to serfdom. Torn from their families and culture, the Indians were forced to work between 14 and 16 hours a day. For indigenous people who had not been exposed to class exploitation, the system of being tied to the land, combined with the diseases brought by the Europeans, was catastrophic. Because the Spaniards brought no women with them, many mestizo children were born to Indian women and, in these early times, most of their descendants were integrated into the European society rather than the indigenous one.

In the first few decades of colonization, Africans, who survived under the system of exploitation better than the Indians did, were brought in as slaves. In small numbers at first, sporadically, and then more steadily, Africans were brought to Cuba, enhancing the racial mixture of the population. Different African cultures quickly began to blend with the nascent Spanish-Indian culture and, by the middle of the 16th century, some of the Cuban nation's present-day cultural features began to emerge.

The Criollo Economy and Society

The island's economy evolved slowly, reflecting the priority Spain gave to its new territories in the Caribbean and South America. At first, Cuba's population decreased when men were sent to participate in the conquest of Mexico and other expeditions, such as that led by Hernando de Soto to Florida. The Spaniards who stayed in Cuba adapted more quickly than expected. In the middle of the 16th century, a new generation of Spanish descendants, most of whom had been born in Cuba, became influential in the nascent colonial world.

During the 16th and 17th centuries and through the first half of the 18th century, cattle ranching remained important, both as providing food for the settlers and as a commodity for trade. Vast cattle ranches covered the island, but these were soon displaced by the development of modern agriculture.

Sown on the banks of rivers, tobacco was a crop that required very little labor, as the Spaniards soon learned from the Indians. Nor did this product require any great capital outlay or large area of land, and the increase in its use in Europe led to a steady growth in demand. In addition, food crops were planted for the settlers, especially those living in Havana. Thus the cattle ranches were replaced by more profitable agriculture. The Spanish government and town councils tried to protect the very powerful group of cattle ranchers, but the Crown's growing need to feed its soldiers and sailors, plus the taxes that agricultural products contributed to the treasury, meant the legislation was rather unclear and disputes between farmers and cattle ranchers filled many a long chapter in Cuba's early history.

Spain's trade monopoly, established through the Casa de Contratación de Sevilla, the king's organization for handling trade with Latin America, weighed particularly heavily on Cuba as Spain failed to supply its colony with the bare necessities. With the creation of the Spanish fleet in 1566, ships began to congregate in the port of Havana, making it the most important port in the New World. The galleons were not supposed to remain there for more than a few weeks, but delays often meant they stayed for months at a time, which stimulated the production and sale of many goods in the settlement of San Cristóbal de La Habana.

The number of inns and taverns also grew apace, promoting the rise of prostitution, especially among black slave women, who were authorized by their owners to "earn" wages. To protect the wealth held in Havana, the mother country built La Punta Fortress and Real Fuerza and Tres Reyes del Morro castles at the entrance to Havana Bay, making the city the best-fortified one in the Americas. The important families whose members served on the town council and who were linked to businesses profiting from the visits of the Spanish fleet began to amass considerable capital, resulting in an economic boom in the 18th century.

Abandoned to their fate, the settlements outside Havana received no benefits from the visiting fleets and quickly turned to smuggling, using hidden coves and rivers as rendezvous points with English, French and Dutch pirates and corsairs, trading local goods for articles not sent by Spain. Both the settlers and the Spanish regional authorities engaged in this contraband trade. The Crown made great—but fruitless— efforts to halt these activities. Melchor Suárez de Poago, the representative of Governor Pedro Valdés, failed to stop the extensive smuggling operations of the people of Bayamo early in the 17th century. This led to legal action that was suspended while being tried in the Crown Court of Santo Domingo.

Corsairs of Spain's enemy nations often attacked Cuba. They included Francis Drake, Francisco Nau, Henry Morgan and Gilberto Girón, who captured Bishop Juan de las Cabezas Altamirano in Bayamo in 1604. The bishop was rescued by a slave in an episode immortalized in *Espejo de Paciencia* (Mirror of Patience), the first poem about Cuba written on the island. To avoid such attacks, Spain tried to impose new administrative controls and approved the transfer of the capital to Havana in 1553.

The island was also divided into two administrative regions: Santiago de Cuba and San Cristóbal de La Habana, with the former subordinated to the latter. Trinidad, Sancti Spíritus and San Juan de los Remedios, the settlements in the middle of the island, were not included in either of these regions, so their inhabitants enjoyed some autonomy for decades. Spain exercised control through such laws as the Cáceres laws, promulgated by Judge Alonso de Cáceres in 1574, which regulated many aspects of Cuba's economic and social life.

The Spanish fleets promoted urban development in Havana, such as the construction of the Main Parish Church between 1550 and 1574 and the Monasteries of Santo Domingo and San Francisco in 1578 and 1584, respectively, and the plan for the Royal Canal in 1592 to provide the settlement with water. There was little progress elsewhere, and only two more important settlements were founded some time later in Santa Clara and Matanzas.

Because of its interest in developing modern agriculture in Cuba, the Spanish monarchy established a state monopoly on tobacco. The Royal Treasury bought the entire year's crop, paying whatever price it chose. Any tobacco it did not buy had to be destroyed. The tobacco growers protested vigorously, but their claims were ignored. Tensions mounted steadily from 1717, culminating in 1723, when the tobacco growers tried to burn down the tobacco warehouses in Havana, an action repressed savagely by Governor Gregorio Guazo who hanged 14 tobacco growers. This was just one of the many clashes that took place between the Spaniards in Spain and those living in the colonies.

By the middle of the 18th century, the monopoly system reached a new stage when the Royal Trading Company of Havana was created with capital contributed by businessmen living in Cuba and in Spain and by the Crown. The company imported and exported all kinds of commodities, including slaves. Shareholders, speculating in production and trade, made considerable profits. This benefited Havana but none of the other settlements. Havana's urban and cultural development continued with the establishment of a Royal Examining Board of Physicians, to supervise the work of dentists, doctors and pharmacists; the arrival of a printing press in 1723; and especially, the founding of the long-desired University of Havana in 1728. With close to 50,000 inhabitants (half of the entire population of Cuba), by 1762 Havana was the principal Spanish city in the Caribbean and Central America.

This was highlighted that same year, when the Family Pact between France and Spain brought Spain into France's war with Britain. Britain decided to seize Havana and landed an expedition of more than 10,000 men a few miles east of the city; after a fierce struggle, they occupied the elevation on which Morro Castle stood, on the eastern side of the entrance to Havana Bay, forcing the city's authorities to surrender.

This placed the western part of Cuba under British rule for close to 11 months. Rather than changing the existing structures, the British made it easier to bring in slaves and this gave an enormous boost to the slave trade, especially with the 13 British colonies in North America, an initial contact that had unexpected consequences in Cuba's later history.

Eventually, Spain recovered its beautiful city by swapping Havana for Florida. The most important aspect of all this was that, while the Spanish authorities did very little to prevent the loss of Havana, its inhabitants and those of neighboring towns—whites, free blacks and slaves—led by José Antonio Gómez (Pepe Antonio), the mayor of Guanabacoa, fought courageously to defend Havana, exhibiting a strong sense of national pride.

After recovering Havana, Spain further strengthened the city by building the huge La Cabaña Fortress next to Morro Castle, thereby indicating Cuba's importance in the forthcoming new era.

Emergence and Evolution of the Plantation System

Slave plantations were the prevailing system of production in Cuba for nearly a century, from the end of the 18th century up to 1886. This system did not originate in Cuba but was already in use on the other islands of the Antilles and especially in the United States and Brazil. This socioeconomic system produced tropical raw materials for the world market, using slave labor that was generally imported from Africa.

Several closely related factors were responsible for the extension of the plantation system in Cuba's specific conditions: the accumulation of capital in the hands of the Havana oligarchy; the "enlightened despotism" of the Spanish monarchy, which adopted more effective methods of rule; the 1804 Haitian revolution, which destroyed the coffee and sugar production of that colony; the fact that Francisco de Arango y Parreño and other key figures who established close relations with the Spanish government were members of the town council of Havana; the law regulating free trade between Spain and the Indies, promulgated in 1778, which liberalized the trade monopoly to some extent; the rapid increase in the numbers of slaves brought to Cuba, a vital stimulus to the economic boom; and the large amount of land still available.

The plantation system spread throughout the eastern and southern parts of what is now Havana province, which had not yet been urbanized, and throughout the areas that are now Havana and Matanzas provinces, as well as Sagua la Grande, Cienfuegos, Trinidad, Santiago de Cuba and Guantánamo. As the plantations spread from west to east, the Havana-Matanzas region was dotted with sugar mills; more sugarcane production meant more blacks, both slaves and freed men and women, more Spaniards, better railroads, and greater scientific advances and cultural development. The traditional cattle ranches were largely replaced by the plantation system, which left its mark on all sectors of Cuban culture and society.

Reform, Annexation and Slavery

Inevitably, the ideology and culture emanating from the plantation system reflected the need to justify and maintain slavery. In Cuba's case, from the theoretical point of view, this promoted reformism. It was a time when most of the Spaniards living in Cuba began to think of themselves as Cubans, and the seeds of the nationalist independence movement that characterized the second half of the 19th century appeared on the plantations, as well as in the towns. Reformist ideas were prevalent between 1790 and 1868, reflecting a wide range of ideas on everything from slavery to Cuba's legal ties to Spain. Reformism, however, was far from homogenous and incorporated many different perspectives.

What were the sources that nourished Cuban reformism? It was informed by the best of Spanish liberal thought (Gaspar Melchor de Jovellanos and Francisco Pi y Margall); Latin America thought that inspired the wars of independence in South America; liberal-bourgeois ideas from the United States had an ever greater influence in Cuba; and, finally, the European bourgeois liberalism that led to the French revolution of 1789. Cuban bourgeois liberalism (or reformism) was never an imitation of trends elsewhere but rather amalgamated and adapted those ideas to Cuba's situation.

Francisco de Arango y Parreño was the main representative of bourgeois reformism in Cuba in the first half of the 19th century. A profound scholar and champion of the European enlightenment, he was a slaveholder who was typical of the growing dissent on the sugarcane plantations. He was proud of being Cuban, although he confused the Spanish homeland with Cuba. For him, Cuba meant a nation of whites, whom he believed embodied the nascent sense of nationality, and he saw the slave trade and plantation system as fundamental to the economic development of the island. He rejected the idea of independence because he thought Cuba could exist under Spanish rule without separating itself from the monarchy. His efforts in Madrid allowed him to obtain significant benefits for the slave-owning sector he represented.

Arango's reformism, therefore, produced very good results up to the time when independence movements developed in South America. The liberation of South America and the end of Spanish enlightened rule with the reign of Ferdinand VII changed Spain's relations with Cuba. Spain now sought to obtain from Cuba the riches lost with the independence of its other South American colonies. Therefore, Madrid granted the captain-general exceptional, all-encompassing powers in 1825 and expelled the Cubans who had been elected deputies to the Cortes in 1837. In the 1830s, Cuba was no longer considered to be an integral part of the Spanish kingdom and was simply viewed as a valuable sugar colony to be exploited. This, along with the maturing of nationalist sentiment among new and broader social sectors in Cuba, meant that the bourgeois reformism of the large slaveholders was replaced by the reformism of other social groups.

The social scientist José Antonio Saco was the best representative of this new wave of reformism. A tenacious champion of Cuban nationalism and daring critic of the flaws of colonialism, Saco was prominent among young intellectuals, such as the educator and philosopher José de la Luz y Caballero. Their ideas were very different from the interests of the large slaveholders and based on the preaching of Bishop Juan José Díaz de Espada, which reflected the burgeoning middle classes in Cuba. The abolition of the slave trade presupposed the eventual end of slavery itself. Criticism of the Spanish government's plantation system helped enormously to awaken various sectors to the evils of colonialism. But Saco left the country in 1834 and Luz y Caballero's health declined, undermining the possible effectiveness of this reformist current in the 1830s.

In the 1870s, bourgeois reformist ideas were revived under Captain-General Francisco Serrano, Duke de la Torre, whose wife came from an important Cuban family. The plantation system was already showing clear symptoms of crisis, and production was increasingly focused on the US market. Thus, the language of the new reformists was more moderate than in earlier eras. Now headed by José Morales Lemus, this group advocated economic and political reforms and the abolition of slavery with compensation for the slaveholders. They presented their views to an Information Council in Madrid in 1866-67; but far from considering their demands, the monarchy imposed a new tax without abolishing the earlier ones. Ignored by the mother country, these Cuban reformists achieved nothing and were superseded in the political arena by those advocating independence.

At one time, within the reformist current, there existed a significant group in favor of Cuba's incorporation into the United States. Annexationism, as it was called, should be considered in the historical context of its time. The level of socioeconomic development attained by the United States, the existence of a strong system of slavery in the southern part of that country and the republican ideology that imbued life in the United States are among the factors that explain why an annexationist movement arose in Cuba (mainly in the western part of the island) between 1840 and 1854.

Narciso López, a Venezuelan who had been a general in the Spanish army and lived in Trinidad (central Cuba), placed himself at the service of the Havana Club to try to block the abolition of slavery. In 1850 and 1851 he led expeditions financed by US Southerners who wanted to influence the balance between slave and non-slave states in the Union in their favor. The only result of these expeditions, tainted as they were by the sordidness of the slave system they espoused, was the creation of a Cuban national flag. López was captured and garroted, and Britain promised Spain it would not demand the abolition of slavery in Cuba; as a result, the annexationist movement went into decline.

Annexationism was a diverse movement. The main group of annexationists were slaveholders in western Cuba who fought tooth and nail to block abolition. In other regions, especially Trinidad and Camagüey, annexationism was motivated by a desire to share in the development and freedoms of the US North, which implied radical abolition. The most important representative of this group of annexationists was the Camagüeyan plantation owner, Joaquín de Agüero, who was executed by the colonial authorities.

Although it was not the predominant trend, a strong independence movement developed during the plantation era. Linked from its beginnings to the emergence of a distinct Cuban national identity, the independence movement was expressed in literature by the poet José María Heredia, who had a lasting influence on Cuban culture and thought.

Social sectors other than those represented by the slaveholders were committed to the creation of a free and independent country. One of their most important actions to achieve this was the conspiracy led by the freed slave José Antonio Aponte in 1812. Inspired by the Haitian revolution, this conspiracy was discovered and ruthlessly crushed. The middle classes organized the Soles y Rayos de Bolívar conspiracy in 1822 and the Gran Legión del Aguila Negra conspiracy in 1829-30, both of which were repressed by the colonial authorities. Nevertheless, these events made it clear that Cuba was no longer immune to the revolutionary movements that had arisen elsewhere in the Americas. These conspiracies also showed the growing strength of the urban middle class, especially in Havana, a city whose population was already more than 120,000 by 1817.

Father Félix Varela y Morales, a professor in Havana, was the main exponent of the independence movement in the first half of the 19th century. Professor of constitutional law at the San Carlos Seminary, a deputy to the Cortes in 1822 and a radical abolitionist, he was persecuted by the king and forced to go into exile in the United States, where he published a pro-independence newspaper, *El Habanero*, between 1824 and 1826. Varela's ethics, his sense of patriotic duty, his support for the independence of South America and the brilliance of his students Saco and Luz made him the most outstanding intellectual of his time.

During the plantation period, a distinctive Cuban culture began to emerge. With Spain as its main influence, this nascent Cuban culture was also open to the best universal achievements from Europe, the Americas and Africa, assimilating what it needed and transforming it into something new and unique. History, pedagogy, literature, music, journalism, economics, demography, architecture, the natural sciences, medicine and philosophy all flourished in Cuba. Prestigious schools trained several generations of future patriots, although it should be noted there were very few schools for black children. In the colonial era, Cuba's national culture reflected the emerging society.

"Cuba wants to be a great, civilized nation, to lend a friendly hand and a fraternal heart to all other peoples."

—Carlos Manuel de Céspedes, 1868

2
The Wars of Independence

"These islands [Cuba and Puerto Rico] are natural appendages of the North American continent.... There are laws of political as well as physical gravitation. And if an apple, severed by the tempest from its native tree, cannot choose but to fall to the ground, Cuba, forcibly disjoined from its own unnatural connection with Spain, and incapable of self support, can gravitate only toward the North American Union, which by the same law of nature cannot cast her off from her bosom."

—John Quincy Adams, US Secretary of State, 1823

The Ten Years' War (1868-78)

The harsh rule by the Spaniards and the maturing of a national feeling fired the Cubans' struggle against the colonial authorities. Rebellions developed in the central and eastern parts of the island led by prominent landowners not linked to the plantation system, who were supported by revolutionary intellectuals and also the campesinos, both black and white. Carlos Manuel de Céspedes, a landowner and lawyer, began an uprising at La Demajagua, in eastern Cuba, on October 10, 1868, which spread rapidly and became known as the Ten Years' War. The main leaders of this rebellion were Ignacio Agramonte, Francisco Vicente Aguilera, Pedro Figueredo, Salvador Cisneros, Máximo Gómez and Antonio Maceo. The original revolutionary program, drawn up by Céspedes, was outlined in the October 10 Manifesto.

Using the tactic of surprise attacks, the rebel forces managed to survive, and several groups of armed men (called *mambís*) met in Guáimaro on April 10 and 11, 1869, and drew up a constitution that established the Republic of Cuba, applying the classical bourgeois division of government into three parts—executive, legislative and judicial—with a military apparatus subordinated to the first. The civilians were not happy with this structure, for they feared it would lead to a system of *caudillismo* that prevailed in the rest of the continent.

Céspedes was elected president of the republic, and a House of Representatives set about drawing up a body of laws to replace the traditional Spanish legislation. After some lukewarm efforts at conciliation, Madrid—experiencing problems arising from the September 1868 revolution in Spain—adopted a policy of "war to the death" from April 1869, reviving the old Corps of Volunteers and making any negotiation between the two belligerents impossible.

With practically no help from abroad, the Cuban rebels gradually gained military experience and confidence in their own strength. Their main historic objectives were to achieve national independence and to abolish slavery. Slavery had apparently been abolished in the Guáimaro constitution of 1869, but was not finally eliminated until December 1870. The struggle against Spain in the countryside made it possible to progressively reduce the gap between black and white Cubans and move toward national integration. In adverse conditions, around 5,000 *mambís* confronted nearly 100,000 Spaniards in an area of 25,000 square miles. The Cubans liberated the rural areas, but Spain retained control in the towns and cities.

The relations between the Cuban executive and legislature turned bitter, especially after Manuel de Quesada was removed as general-in-chief in December 1869. Quesada, the president's brother-in-law, was removed by the House of Representatives when he requested greater freedom for the military apparatus, and his post was never filled. Subsequently, each general began to act independently, taking whatever measures he thought necessary in his region. The Cubans living in the United States, who were weakened by internal squabbles, sent very little help to the *mambís*. Céspedes sent Quesada north as his personal emissary, and the émigrés split into two groups: those in favor of Quesada (the Quesadistas) and those who followed the Havana plantation owner Miguel Aldama (the Aldamistas). Even the arrival of Cuba's Vice-President, Francisco Vicente Aguilera, failed to settle the quarrel.

Several Latin American nations expressed their support for the Republic of Cuba. Even though the region's limited economic development restricted its expression in material form, many young Latin Americans came to Cuba to fight for its freedom. They included Juan Rius Rivera, from Puerto Rico, and José Rogelio Castillo, from Colombia, both of whom rose to the rank of general.

In line with the United States' traditional interest in Cuba, US President Ulysses S. Grant did not recognize the Cubans' struggle for independence and hindered their patriotic work in the United States. He denounced the Cuban war in his annual messages to Congress; and helped Spain by passing on all the information available to him. In 1874, Secretary Hamilton Fish blocked an excellent Colombian plan that proposed purchasing Cuba's independence from Madrid with contributions from all the other Latin American nations. Throughout the war, the United States supported leaving Cuba in Spanish hands until it could acquire the island for itself.

Several events during the first five years of the war were key. First, Máximo Gómez advanced his troops into the Guantánamo region in 1871; then, the same year, the Spaniards put eight Havana medical students before a firing squad, having falsely accused them of desecrating a Spaniard's tomb. Ignacio Agramonte died in 1873 and Céspedes was removed as president, due to differences with the House of Representatives; he died the following year. General Calixto García was captured and several major battles took place in 1874 led by Máximo Gómez, the top-ranking *mambí* general, at Naranjo, Mojacasabe and Las Guásimas, in the Camagüey area. To a certain extent, the vicissitudes in Spain's domestic political scene—the monarchy, republicanism and the restoration of Alfonso XII—facilitated the rebels' achievements.

Early in 1875, with fewer than 2,000 men, Máximo Gómez, the rebel military chief in Camagüey and Las Villas provinces, began to move westward as a first step toward extending the war. The *mambís* crossed the Trocha—a string of Spanish military fortifications from Júcaro to Morón that divided Cuba in two—and burned many sugar mills and farms, applying a scorched-earth policy. At the same time, they freed all the slaves they encountered. The colonial power in Cuba began to crumble. Internal problems, however, prevented the rebels from continuing the campaign.

Gómez had asked the House of Representatives to send reinforcements as he began to move his troops west. When the time came, these reinforcements were called to a meeting at Lagunas de Varona (in what is now Las Tunas province), by supporters of General Vicente García and his friends, relatives of Céspedes (who had been removed as president). The soldiers were reluctant to leave their own provinces and go to Las Villas and they demanded, among other things, that the civilian leadership replace President Cisneros, modify the constitution and hold an election.

The weakness of the executive and legislative branches of the government was shown by their failure to take drastic measures against this sedition. Instead, they asked Gómez to meet with General García. During their meeting, Gómez and García agreed to appoint Juan Bautista Spotorno as interim president. The presidency was then assumed by Tomás Estrada Palma in 1876. The unity among the revolutionaries was shattered, and the troops' advance toward the west was halted. This betrayal was a factor in the death of the head of the vanguard, a US citizen named Henry Reeve, who was called "El Inglesito," or "the little Englishman."

Regionalism, which had historically characterized Cuban life and politics throughout the colonial period, had taken root in the combatants from Las Villas to such an extent that, in October 1876, speaking on behalf of the Las Villas officers, Carlos Roloff, a Pole, asked Máximo Gómez to step down as head of the region. This deeply upset Gómez, and he returned to Camagüey at a moment when revolutionary unity was crucial, in view of appointment of Arsenio Martínez Campos as the new Spanish captain-general.

Martínez Campos was known in Spain as "the Pacifier" because of his successful intervention in that country's serious political and military disputes. He had graduated from a military academy and had already taken part in the Cuban war, introducing both military and nonmilitary tactics. For example, he proposed returning the goods seized from the large Cuban landowners; he guaranteed that *mambís* who surrendered would not be killed and, if necessary, gave them some money; he did away with deportations; he distributed food to starving combatants; and generally he succeeded in destroying the rebels' power base throughout Cuba. At that critical point in the war, this policy brought excellent results.

The *mambí* government tried to solve the crisis by appointing General Vicente García to take command in Las Villas. He prevaricated and initiated a new act of military sedition in May 1877. Deciding not to follow the government's orders, García returned to Las Tunas, his usual area of operations. The fighting had almost ended in central Cuba and the executive had again fallen into crisis when President Estrada Palma was captured in November 1877. Francisco Javier de Céspedes served as interim president for a short time, and then the House of Representatives appointed Vicente García as president to save the republic.

Several factors combined to lead to a peace accord at Zanjón Farm on February 10, 1978, that failed to bring independence. Nearly 10 years of fighting had exhausted the country and the rebels had received very little war materiel from abroad. The lack of unity, the personal ambition of many leaders, the lack of an army with a strong central command, the ineptness of the apparatus of the revolutionary government, which, far from facilitating, hindered the war operations; and finally the confusion among some of the chiefs about the relations between civil power and the military command were all factors contributing to the defeat. Martínez Campos took advantage of this situation. The Zanjón Pact, which ended the Ten Years' War, recognized the freedom of the slaves and Chinese coolies who had joined the *mambí* ranks, promised to grant liberal-bourgeois reforms (although this promise was not kept) and declared the agreement effective throughout Cuba.

In spite of his sagacity, the Spanish military leader was astounded when the *mambís* in eastern Cuba led by General Antonio Maceo (a mulatto with tremendous prestige at the end of the war), refused to accept the agreement. In a memorable meeting in March 1878 at Mangos de Baraguá, near the Sierra Maestra mountains, the *mambíses* declared their determination to continue the fight. They created a new government and proclaimed yet another revolutionary constitution. Although this only lasted for a few months (due to their chronic lack of resources and the concentration of all Spain's troops against them), the *mambíses* became an example of Cuban intransigence and the refusal to accept colonial status.

By the middle of the year 1878, the first stage of Cuba's wars of independence had ended without the creation of an independent government or a nation state; nevertheless, considerable political-military experience had been gained that would be useful in later efforts. Few *mambí* fighters returned to their homes in Cuba; the vast majority of them went abroad, where the struggle for Cuba's independence was now centered.

The Period Between the Wars

The last quarter of the 19th century saw the development of capitalism in Cuba, and Cuban society as it would be in the next century began to take shape.

A growing concentration of productive forces became apparent in the second half of the century. The less efficient sugar mills—those that had failed to modernize—disappeared, giving way to new industries. Many of the producers who lost their sugar mills dedicated themselves to planting sugarcane to be ground in other mills. Thus, the division between the agricultural and industrial aspects of sugar production appeared.

Moreover, because Spain did not consume very much sugar, the Cuban sugar market became increasingly oriented to the United States, so that by 1895 Cuba sold over 85 percent of its sugar to its northern neighbor.

Moreover, US sugar importers and sellers had stopped buying refined Cuban sugar, preferring to purchase raw, unprocessed sugar. As a consequence, sugar refining in Cuba dropped off sharply, and the colony was reduced to the status of a producer of raw materials. Even though Spain's domestic market was small, it had demanded refined sugar. Now Cuba's sugarcane industry became more and more subordinated to the US market and its demands.

The United States began to invest capital in the island and, by the end of the century, those investments—mainly in sugar and mining—amounted to close to $50 million. Henry Havemeyer's creation of the Sugar Trust in 1891 tightened the chains of dependence on the United States, separating Cuba further from Spain and did much to subordinate the formerly powerful Cuban bourgeoisie.

The weakness of the Cuban economy and its dependence on the United States were highlighted when business groups on the island asked Spain to sign a reciprocal trade agreement with the United States to guarantee that market. But this agreement was never ratified. In 1890, the United States applied more pressure on other nations in the Americas with the McKinley Bill and its corollary, the Aldrich Amendment, which closed the US market to those countries that did not open their doors to industrial products from the United States. Spain's stubborn refusal to reduce tariffs on US products gave rise to the Economic Movement in Cuba, a group of producers and sellers who joined together to defend their interests. Even though that movement did not achieve all its goals, it did highlight the dependent nature of the Cuban economy.

With the development of capitalism, it became necessary to abolish slavery. In 1880, after long consultations with the slaveholders, Madrid issued the Trust Law, which extended slavery for eight years; but, in fact, slavery was abolished sooner in 1886. The newly freed black slaves swelled the ranks of the agricultural work force. But the shortage of field hands remained a constant problem for Cuban agriculture into the 20th century. Abolition, however, contributed significantly to enlarging the domestic market.

Under the measures proposed by Martínez Campos at Zanjón, a process of creating political parties began in 1878. The result was the formation of two large groups, the Constitutional Union and Liberal Autonomist parties. The former represented the interests of the big Spanish producers and merchants who had managed to modernize. This group also included quite a few Cubans. Politically intransigent and allies of Madrid, they advocated Cuba's "assimilation" into Spain.

The Liberal Autonomist Party represented the less powerful elements of the Cuban ruling class, supported by prominent intellectuals. Since most of its members had been born in Cuba, this party considered itself the representatives of national interests. Its leading figures were professionals such as José María Gálvez, José Antonio Cortina, Miguel Figueroa and Rafael Montoro. They campaigned for two decades on the political platform of autonomy. The autonomists had a strong economic foundation and some commitment to improving the lot of the Cuban masses, and they attracted a following for some time. The brilliant oratory of some of the autonomists highlighted the problems of the colonial regime without going so far as to advocate independence, ultimately simply proposing modest reforms to the status quo.

Spain failed to recognize or exploit autonomism and the fact that it represented the postponement of the independence struggle. It sought to preserve its national traditions and way of life, holding fraudulent elections, revising laws to benefit itself and hindering the propaganda of the autonomists, who were marginalized from the governmental apparatus. Autonomism lost much of its support as the independence movement revived and disenchantment with Spain grew. By 1893, autonomism had failed to get Spain to implement any reforms in Cuba and the way was clear for a new stage in the struggle for the creation of an independent nation state.

After the Ten Years' War, those supporting independence did not give up, but set about preparing for what became known as the Little War (1879-80). But failing to make an objective analysis of the causes of their earlier defeat, the independentista groups were not structured horizontally. They had a center in New York that was directed by Calixto García, but some of the rebel groups in Cuba did not coordinate their activities with other groups or with the center. Thus, the war quickly ran out of steam due to a lack of resources and because of the differences between García and Antonio Maceo. The Liberal Autonomist Party supported Spain, arguing this was a war of blacks against whites. The Little War ended in October 1880, its most significant legacy being the emergence of José Martí Pérez, Cuba's future national hero.

Isolated expeditions were organized during the 1880s to spark another war of independence, but they were not very well organized or successful, in spite of the role of leaders such as Generals Carlos Agüero, Limbano Sánchez and Ramón Leocadio Bonachea. The best-prepared plan of this period led by General Máximo Gómez between 1884 and 1886 also failed. The independence movement did not yet understand the objective and subjective forces required for a revolution or the need to create effective unity among the revolutionaries before beginning a war against the colonial power.

The War of 1895

There was a man who had not been demoralized in the previous struggles for independence and who made unity among the combatants the top priority; he placed the movement on a new foundation with a truly radical ideological platform. That man, José Martí, was born of Spanish parents and lived in exile in the United States after having spent several very productive years in Spain, Mexico, Guatemala and Venezuela. By the 1890s, he was the most famous writer in the Spanish language and the most prominent journalist in the Americas.

This new stage of the independence movement was distinguished by a comprehensive socioeconomic program for the development of Cuba and a strong organizational base. The revolutionary program promoted by Martí had taken shape among the Cuban émigrés of the Cuban Revolutionary

Party (PRC), which was founded on April 10, 1892. Through the PRC and its newspaper, *Patria*, Martí effectively campaigned to promote social change in Cuba and unity of the independentistas behind the PRC and himself as its delegate. In September 1892 the unification process reached an important milestone when General Máximo Gómez accepted supreme command of the revolutionary military forces in the forthcoming battles.

Little by little, key figures were won over to Martí's program. They included Generals Serafín Sánchez, José Rogelio Castillo, José Maceo, Flor Crombet and, of course, Antonio Maceo. Martí did not call for a civilian government like that in 1878; rather, he offered a definitive solution for the conflicts that had arisen between the civilian and military authorities in the past wars. This was combined with Latin Americanist ideas that the working masses and other nationalist sectors of society could use to prevent the United States from expanding throughout what Martí called "Our America."[1]

On February 24, 1895, Guillermo Moncada and Bartolomé Masó led uprisings against the colonial authorities in the eastern part of Cuba that lasted for some weeks. Martí's plan of simultaneous uprisings and expeditions failed for several reasons, but Martí revised the plan and went to Santo Domingo, where he wrote the programmatic document known as the *Manifesto of Montecristi*,[2] which he and Gómez signed. After many vicissitudes, they managed to land in Cuba at Cajobabo Beach, in Oriente province, in April 1895. General Maceo had landed at Duaba a few days earlier and had immediately

---

1. José Martí, Letter to Manuel Mercado, in *José Martí Reader*, (Ocean Press, 2007), pp 253-56.

2. José Martí, "Manifesto of Montecristi," in *José Martí Reader*, (Ocean Press, 2007), pp 190-200.

assumed military command of the eastern province. (Generals Moncada and Crombet had both died recently.)

Martí and Gómez met with Maceo at La Mejorana Farm on May 5. Martí and General Gómez had similar views on the civilian revolutionary organization, but Maceo did not entirely agree. A few days later, on May 19, José Martí was killed in combat near Dos Ríos; thus the anti-colonial struggle lost both its best ideologue and one of the greatest intellectuals in the Americas. Gómez and Maceo agreed to extend the war throughout Oriente province (eastern Cuba). Maceo won battles at Jobito, Peralejo and Sao del Indio, and Gómez went to Camagüey where, with the support of Salvador Cisneros, he waged his famous circular campaign around the city of Puerto Príncipe, as his green troops became accustomed to battle. A few weeks later, a large expedition of men under the command of Serafín Sánchez and Carlos Roloff landed on the southern coast of Las Villas province.

A constitutional assembly in the Jimaguayú area, in Camagüey province, in September approved a constitution that tried to achieve a fair balance between civil and military authorities and established a six-person Governing Council with legislative and executive functions. Salvador Cisneros was elected president, and Bartolomé Masó, vice-president. The Assembly ratified Gómez and Maceo in their posts and appointed Tomás Estrada Palma foreign minister. Estrada was also the delegate of the Cuban Revolutionary Party, a post he had held since the death of José Martí.

The next step was to prepare for the advance westward, which began at Mangos de Baraguá with Gómez as commander-in-chief and Maceo second-in-command. This was one of the most brilliant military campaigns in the history of the Americas. In a very small area, a few hundred poorly armed and hungry *mambís* confronted a well-supplied Spanish army with great combat ability and, in just three months, the Cubans advanced more than 600 miles, sometimes 50 miles at a time. Clashes occurred at Iguará, Mal Tiempo, Coliseo, Calimete and Lazo de la Invasión. The *mambís* reached Havana province in January 1896, and it was agreed that Maceo should conclude the campaign by going to Pinar del Río province, in the westernmost part of the country, while Gómez would keep enemy troops busy in Havana province. The accord marking the completion of the undertaking was signed in Mantua, in western Cuba, on January 22, 1896.

Spain decided to take extreme measures and replaced Martínez Campos with Valeriano Weyler. Already resident in Cuba and representing reactionary colonial interests, Weyler applied a genocidal policy of "reconcentration," forcing campesinos into urban areas to prevent them from helping the *mambís*. (This same policy was employed by the British against Boer women and children in South Africa around this time.) Those in the concentration camps lacked all the necessities of life; the sick were left to die, and the figures for the sick and dead were horrendous. Between 150,000 and 200,000 people died in 1896 and 1897. Nevertheless, the war continued.

In addition to the many combatants and civilian casualties, many revolutionary leaders died during the first few years of the war, including Guillermón Moncada, Flor Crombet, Francisco Borrero, Juan Bruno Zayas, José María Aguirre, José Maceo, Serafín Sánchez and Antonio Maceo, second-in-command of the *mambí* army, who was killed in battle at San Pedro, Havana province, in December 1896. In spite of these losses, Commander-in-Chief Máximo Gómez continued to lead the *mambí* troops without significant losses of men.

Revolutionary unity was threatened by conflicts between the Governing Council and the commander-in-chief. The former, seeking to control the officers, soon began to interfere in military matters by making military appointments, tolerating commerce with the enemy, and, above all, allowing sugarcane to be milled in order to meet the agreements Estrada Palma had made abroad. This led to serious friction with Gómez, whom the civilian authority accused of "interfering" in the life of the republic. The *mambí* chief resigned, but the deaths of Maceo and of his aide, Francisco Gómez, Máximo Gómez's son, led to an easing of these tensions. Meanwhile, the autonomists took advantage of these difficulties to influence the course of the war.

After Maceo's death, Calixto García was promoted to second-in-command, and he led outstanding campaigns in Oriente using artillery. Gómez, who was determined to wear Spain down, set up camp in the La Reforma area, between Las Villas and Camagüey provinces and, exploiting the tropical heat, exhausted 40,000 Spanish soldiers, leading them a merry chase. After several weeks, this policy bore fruit: thousands of Spanish soldiers were hospitalized, and Spain had no way to replace them.

To fully understand the War of 1895, the plans various US administrations had had for Cuba should not be forgotten. Britain had always had its eye on Cuba and, because Spain was a weaker imperialist power than Britain, Washington was afraid that the island would fall into English hands, preferring that it remain a Spanish colony. But taking advantage of the international situation, in 1896 US President Grover Cleveland began to pressure Spain to end the conflict. His successor, William McKinley, stepped up these demands. Inventing "war news," the yellow press whipped up public opinion in the United States, playing on the US people's sympathy for Cuba's independence.

As the delegate of the Cuban Revolutionary Party, Estrada Palma abandoned his principles and tried to bring about the end of the fighting by proposing the United States either purchase Cuba or intervene militarily. This would protect the ruling class's economic interests and avoid a revolution of the masses. Yielding to Washington, Spain pretended to end the concentration camps, removed Weyler and installed Ramón Blanco as the head of a fictional Autonomous administration in 1898. The Liberal Autonomist Party acceded to this, although its members fell into bitter argument. In this situation, autonomism was no solution to Cuba's problems, and the *mambís* energetically opposed it.

In response to the *mambís'* protests, the groups of volunteers who were closely linked to the recalcitrant defenders of Spanish traditions and way of life invited the US government, which was expressing "concern" over what might happen to the citizens of Havana, to send the battleship *Maine*. In February 1898, the ship was blown up in Havana Bay—an event that is still the subject of much conjecture—triggering accusations by both the United States and Spain. In response, President McKinley first offered to purchase the island and then asked US Congress to declare war.

On April 20, after much lobbying by Cuban officials close to Estrada Palma, the US Senate and the House of Representatives passed a Joint Resolution that recognized Cuba's independence and stated that the United States would turn the island over to its people once peace was restored, without seeking to annex it. In the future, this resolution would become an obstacle to US plans for Cuba, but at the time it enabled the United States to intervene in Cuba's war against Spain.

Because of domestic political conflicts, Spain felt obliged to take up the gauntlet against the much stronger nation, and the war with the United States lasted from May to August 1898.

In line with their usual stance, the US authorities ignored Cuba's Governing Council and the Liberation Army. Máximo

Gómez was completely pushed aside. Nevertheless the Governing Council led by Bartolomé Masó—who had been elected president after the adoption of the Constitution of La Yaya in October 1897—ordered the *mambís* in eastern Cuba not to abandon the theater of operations, and they continued the struggle alongside US troops. Calixto García drew up plans for seizing Santiago de Cuba—a feat that the US high command thought to be impossible. General García and his *mambí* troops were rewarded by the North Americans for accomplishing this brilliant achievement by being prevented entering Santiago de Cuba, supposedly in order to avoid possible reprisals. The Joint Resolution was thus trampled underfoot.

When the Spaniards finally surrendered, their pride meant they preferred to surrender to the US troops rather than to the Cubans. The United States had had everything in its favor, and the US squadron had sunk the weak remnants of the Spanish navy in the battle of Santiago de Cuba. That battle determined the later course of events and enabled the United States to take possession of Cuba, Puerto Rico and the Philippines with very little effort.

The naval blockade imposed by Washington had done a lot of damage to Cuba, and the cease-fire in August 1898 aggravated the situation. Food seized by the rebels was considered contraband. Following their instructions to help the weak against the stronger, the North American occupiers distributed food to the Spaniards.

Meanwhile, complying with the provisions of the Constitution of La Yaya, the Cuban leaders dissolved the Governing Council and called for an election to be held in October to choose the members of a new body, the Assembly of Santa Cruz, which was moved first to Marianao and then to Cerro on the outskirts of Havana in 1899. Abroad, Estrada

Palma dissolved the Cuban Revolutionary Party, and that was the end of José Martí's beloved organization.

On December 10, 1898, representatives of Spain and the United States met in Paris to sign a peace treaty that brought an end to the war. No representatives of the Cuban people were allowed to participate. Considering Cuba's uncertain status, Máximo Gómez commented that his homeland was neither free nor independent. The threat to Cuba's national identity and the danger of annexation by a foreign power were evident. The end of European colonialism in no way meant the creation of a nation state.

Fortunately, the Cuban people had a long tradition of struggle and a commitment to independence that sustained them when, on January 1, 1899, the United States intervened for the first time after Cuba's "independence." Even though the US forces of occupation were very powerful, they found it difficult to prevent the establishment of a republic in the Pearl of the Antilles.

"Once the United States is in Cuba, who will get it out?"

—José Martí, 1889

3
Republic and Sovereignty

"Of course, Cuba has very little or no independence left after the Platt Amendment... I believe it is a very desirable acquisition for the United States. The island will gradually become North American and, in due time, we will have one of the richest and most desired possessions in the world."

—Leonard Wood, military governor of Cuba 1899-1902

The First Period of US Intervention

On January 1, 1899, a new era opened in Cuba—the era of US intervention. After four centuries of rule, the Spanish colonialists left Cuba without creating an independent nation state and—even worse—with the Cuban people having no clear idea of their future. Even though the Joint Resolution supported the Cubans' right to full sovereignty, it seemed likely that the US government would take advantage of the situation, especially considering the state of the revolutionary, patriotic forces. The Assembly of Santa Cruz and the *mambí* army had no experience that helped them understand the demands of the historic new situation. And as usual, subjective disputes arose among the patriots and they were soon subsumed by internal squabbles.

In January 1899, the United States had no clearly defined policy on Cuba. Many diverse forces had conflicting interests. Some advocated maintaining Cuba as a colony while others favored annexation as a means of controlling the island. Others sincerely supported Cuba's independence. Gradually, Cuba's domestic situation led to the creation of a new republic tightly bound to the United States.

General John R. Brooke was the first US military governor of Cuba and he acted in this role until December 1899. Not belonging to any of the groups that strongly advocated annexation, Brooke surrounded himself with figures who had been involved in the war and created a four-member civilian cabinet to assist him. He commenced a process of making the island more like the United States. An effort was made to put the economy and other sectors on a sound footing, and an Anglo-Saxon style of education was promoted, including the introduction of English in schools. In addition, many young people went to the United States where they took teacher training courses.

A census taken to ascertain the real size of the population and state of the economy showed that Cuba had around 1,572,000 inhabitants. In 1900, a police force and its rural equivalent, the Rural Guards, were created.

When the war ended, the *mambí* army was terribly short of resources, forcing the revolutionary leadership, with no clear view of the future, to dissolve the army and help its members return to their homes, mainly in the rural areas. The Assembly now based in Cerro hoped to obtain a US governmental loan that would give it official recognition. But Commander-in-Chief Máximo Gómez preferred instead to accept a donation offered by the wily McKinley.

Tempers became heated and the Assembly sacked Gómez. This proved counterproductive because Gómez retained broad support among the Cuban people. The Assembly broke up in early April, and the *mambí* army received a "gift" of $3 million, to be distributed proportionally among its members. In one stroke, the disunity among the revolutionary forces enabled the US government to dismantle the last two representative bodies that had existed since the War of 1895, leaving the Cuban people leaderless.

Political parties had begun to emerge in 1899. Both the revolutionaries and others organized themselves with a view to taking part in future elections. Many small groups appeared that later merged with stronger organizations, such as the Cuban National Party, the Federal Republican Party of Havana, the Federal Republican Party of Las Villas and the Democratic

Union. Gómez tried to unite the former *mambís* into a single, powerful party, but this effort failed due to sectarianism.

The emerging political parties were generally gathered around various caudillos and did not represent the specific interests of particular social classes on the island or offer different programs. Here, again, the independence forces lost an opportunity to consolidate themselves.

Leonard Wood replaced Brooke as military governor in December 1899. Much more aggressive than his predecessor, Wood promoted the United States' annexation of Cuba, but this was opposed by the vast majority of the Cuban people, who wanted the island to become an independent republic. This hindered the creation of a civilian government and showed Washington the need to come up with a solution that, while strongly binding Cuba to its northern neighbor, proclaimed a new nation in the Caribbean. Therefore, municipal elections with very limited franchise were held, followed by a general election on July 25, 1900, to select the delegates to a Constitutional Assembly.

This Constitutional Assembly met from November 15, 1900, to February 1901, approving a constitution that was the product of a compromise among the representatives and did not express the Cuban people's most ardent desire for independence; rather, it reflected the liberal legislative tradition of a government consisting of three powers.

Wood's instructions to the members of the Constitutional Assembly called for the definition in the constitution of the special relationship between Cuba and the United States. The vast majority of the members of the Assembly rejected this and said so, but the US government was not about to permit Cuba to have full sovereignty and told the Cubans that, if they did not accept the conditions laid down by Senator Orville Platt in his famous amendment to the appropriations bill for the US Army, there would be no Cuban republic. In June 1901, after considerable discussion in the Constitutional Assembly on the question of national sovereignty, the Amendment was approved by a vote of 16 to 11.

Article III of the Amendment curtailed Cuba's sovereignty, giving the United States the right to intervene in Cuba's internal affairs whenever it deemed this necessary. Article VII allowed the United States to maintain naval bases and coaling stations in Cuba, either through buying or leasing them. After the Amendment was approved, the Cuban patriotic forces began a tenacious struggle to revoke it, a struggle that continued for two decades.

Tomás Estrada Palma and Bartolomé Masó were the presidential candidates in 1901. The former, who had a moderate political background and the blessing of the United States, had very solid support. Masó had fewer followers, and certainly less charisma, but he was a dedicated patriot who opposed the Platt Amendment. US pressure forced Masó to withdraw his nomination, so Estrada Palma was elected unopposed. This led to a worsening of the traditional splits among the independence forces.

Thus, everything was ready for the United States to withdraw its troops from Cuba, which it did after two important military orders were left as proof of the United States' real intentions. The first military order (number 34) facilitated penetration of Cuba by US railroad companies, while the second military order (number 62) called for surveying formerly communal lands, making it easier for US investors to acquire land. Only then, after Cuba's future sovereignty had been seriously compromised by the Platt Amendment and the first president had been elected, did the forces of occupation withdraw from the island. On May 20, 1902, the neocolonial, truncated Republic of Cuba was officially proclaimed.

From Tomás Estrada Palma to Gerardo Machado

President Estrada Palma and his government were faced with a tremendous challenge. On the one hand, they had to rebuild a nation destroyed by the war against Spain, in which poverty, unemployment, illiteracy and the results of Spanish neglect were evident throughout the country. On the other, they had to mobilize the patriotic elements to obtain the greatest sovereignty possible within the narrow limits that the Platt Amendment allowed.

This required great national unity around the republican project and the integration of the heterogeneous political sectors of the island were required, but Estrada Palma was not the right man for the job. His views on the advantages of foreign guardianship over Cuba, at least during the first few years of independence, and his distance from the masses of the Cuban people made him far from ideal for leading the nation in that period, as was soon shown.

Moreover, the Cuban oligarchy was incapable of acting in the national interest, and did not even try to do so. Rather, it contented itself with the space left by US capital, whose influence steadily increased over the next several decades. The dependent nature of the Cuban economy, especially the sugar industry, acted as a brake on the development of the republic. Sugar served as the spearhead for foreign penetration, working against the more progressive sectors of the economy.

A reciprocal trade agreement between Cuba and the United States was hurriedly drafted and approved in December 1902; it was ratified the next year. This agreement proposed both countries reduce their tariffs by 20 percent, but Cuban tariffs were often reduced by 40 percent, showing how unreciprocal the agreement was. The island's production of raw materials for the US market was guaranteed, in exchange for which it could purchase large quantities of the United States' industrial products.

Even though, at first, the agreement helped to create new jobs, in the medium term it consolidated Cuba's status as an importer, with a single-crop economy and a single export crop, completely dependent on a single market, and more and more subjected to the dictates of the United States. While sugar constituted 36 percent of all Cuba's exports in 1900, it accounted for close to 84 percent of its exports in 1925, thanks to this agreement.

The Estrada Palma administration worked hard to establish the new republic, signing treaties that Washington considered absolutely necessary: the 1903 Permanent Treaty—that is, the Platt Amendment, now signed by a Cuban government; a 1903 agreement on leasing naval bases and coaling stations, which was modified later on; and the 1904 Treaty on the Isle of Pines, that recognized Cuban sovereignty over the smaller island but which was not ratified by the US government until 1925. All these pacts confirmed agreements entered into during the first period of US intervention.

Rather than dedicating himself to the development of the new nation's economy within the set limits, President Estrada Palma tried to make the best possible use of the government's precious resources, with a view to paying off the $35 million loan that US private capital had supplied. Inevitably, this hindered implementation of badly needed social reforms, so he soon lost popular support. At the same time, the political groups backing Estrada Palma formed the Moderate Party, which later became the Conservative Party, to oppose the Liberal Party, which had deep-rooted popular support. Convinced it was his "patriotic" duty, Estrada Palma launched his reelection campaign in 1905. His main opponent was

Máximo Gómez; but unfortunately Gómez died in June of that same year.

Largely through fraud, Estrada Palma was reelected, and this resulted in widespread public protests, which were violently suppressed. The Liberals, led by General José Miguel Gómez and Alfredo Zayas, rose up in arms in the Little War of August 1906. The uprising endangered the precarious republican system and gave the United States a pretext for applying Article III of the Platt Amendment. Former *mambís* and political leaders convinced President Estrada Palma to resign. Members of cabinet and the heads of the legislative bodies also resigned. Once again, Cuba was bereft of leadership and, in September 1906, the US government announced it was intervening in Cuba again.

This intervention differed from the former one in many ways. Most important, this time, Cuba was a republic and the US government had to acknowledge this. Understood to be temporary, the occupation lasted until 1909. Charles Magoon, a lawyer and former administrator of the Panama Canal, became Cuba's provisional governor. He strengthened relations with the Liberal groups that Estrada Palma had displaced and established a Consultative Commission of prestigious jurists in December 1906 to draw up laws to complement the 1901 Constitution.

A new census was taken in 1907, indicating that Cuba now had nearly 2.1 million inhabitants—an enormous increase over the number in 1899. Havana had a population of 300,000, and the number of foreigners—mainly Spaniards, Haitians and Jamaicans—was steadily increasing.

Magoon also took it upon himself to create a national standing army for the first time in Cuba's history. The legacy of Magoon's administration, which was as colorless as the man himself, was the embezzlement of the money that Estrada

Palma had left in the treasury, conservatively estimated at around 11 million pesos, and the dizzying spread of administrative corruption with the granting of sinecures, a political practice that had flourished in the Spanish colonial era.

Displaced by the Moderates in 1905, the Liberals were confident they would win the 1908 election. José Miguel Gómez, with Zayas as his running mate, won a landslide victory and became president in January 1909, thus bringing to a close the second period of US intervention.

The Liberal administration included well-respected patriots, and Cubans expected them to do much more than Estrada Palma. Furthermore, President Gómez was a man of undeniable charisma, a farmer who had become a rebel major-general and who was regarded a true representative of the poor. But almost immediately, José Miguel Gómez showed himself to be just the opposite.

The Liberal administration, from 1909 to 1913, became notorious for corruption. Drawing on the treasury as if it were their personal property, President Gómez and his coterie stole, and permitted others to steal, enormous sums from the profits contributed to the public coffers by growing US investments. Not content with asking for and getting a loan of $16.5 million from US banks, fraudulent dealings became commonplace—such as the swapping of the Arsenal land for the Villanueva land in January 1910, which put a lot of money into the pockets of important members of the regime; the granting of the concession for dredging the ports in February 1911, with payments of millions to those involved; and the supposed draining of the Zapata Swamp in June 1912, which was assigned to an incompetent US company and was never carried out. Such fraud became public and led to bitter criticism in the Cuban press. Expectations that the Liberals would tackle the nation's problems were dashed.

Reacting to the discrimination they suffered, Afro-Cubans tried to organize a political party called Independents of Color. Congress quickly passed a law prohibiting groups organized on the basis of race, among other classifications. The Afro-Cubans, many of whom were former *mambís*, brought pressure to bear on the government to legalize their party and, when they failed, made the mistake of taking up arms in May 1912, hoping that their former comrade José Miguel Gómez would sympathize with them.

Afraid of being accused of being weak and very aware of the possible threat contained in Article III of the Platt Amendment, President Gómez ordered the massacre of the rebels, who, since they had very few weapons, offered little resistance to the combined forces of the army and the Rural Guards. This uprising of the independence forces became the most tragic episode in the history of the Liberal administration. Moreover, with its new policy of preventing trouble before it arose, Washington landed a group of Marines in Oriente province, the main region involved in the uprising.

Refusing to support the presidential aspirations of his vice-president Zayas (the leader of an important Liberal faction), José Miguel Gómez backed the Conservatives, led by *mambí* General Mario García Menocal. As the former manager of the US-owned Chaparra Sugar Mill, Menocal had Washington's approval. He had studied engineering in the United States and was a born elitist. Energetic, a lover of Anglo-Saxon customs and habits and a bitter enemy of radical social or economic reforms, Menocal came to power in 1913, riding a wave of anti-Liberalism. His authoritarianism did not take long to reveal itself.

How he came to remain in power between 1913 and 1921—for two presidential terms—is explained by the fact that World War I broke out in 1914 and the United States played an important part in that conflagration. President Menocal followed suit and also declared war on Germany. Sugar became a key war materiel, and Cuba was the United States' main supplier. Menocal was able to get away with what Estrada Palma and José Miguel Gómez had not, because at this point the United States needed a "strong man" who would accept US dictates in governing Cuba.

As the war progressed, the demand for sugar grew ever greater, and the price rose. Washington therefore turned a blind eye to Menocal's scandalous electoral fraud that ensured his reelection in 1916. Resorting to the methods that had proved so useful in 1906, his opponent, José Miguel Gómez, led an armed uprising against Menocal in various parts of the country in February 1917. Known as La Chambelona, this gave rise to the contagious conga that has been popular in Cuba ever since. The United States made it very clear that it would not support the uprising, which simply fizzled out after leaving several dozen Cubans dead.

Some groups of US Marines were landed at this time as a preventive measure. In an attempt to avoid further electoral problems in Cuba, the US government also sent Enoch Crowder to Havana to modify the electoral laws, a task he completed by August 1919.

Acceding to a longstanding demand, Menocal established a national currency, which went into circulation in 1914. He arranged for several loans of close to $50 million from US banks and also organized another census in 1919, which, like the previous one, showed a considerable population increase (this time, to around 2.9 million people). The number of foreigners continued to rise with the growth of sugar and urban development, reaching an excessive level for an agricultural country. Havana, with a population of close to 400,000 inhabitants, was the most important city in Central

America and the Caribbean. Under President Menocal, Havana grew at a great pace as the sugar barons built mansions in the city. In this period, women began to organize to achieve the vote, founding the Women's Club of Cuba in 1918.

In cooperation with the United States' war effort and in spite of resistance by the Cuban sugar producers, in 1917 the Cuban government agreed the United States could purchase the entire sugarcane harvest for 4.6 cents a pound—a price that, while reasonable, was lower than the market price. This was repeated the next year, although the purchase price of sugar rose to 5.5 cents a pound.

Even though Menocal's gesture—made in gratitude for the support the United States had given to his reelection—meant a loss of hundreds of millions of dollars, the sugarcane harvests, which were increasing at a rapid rate and had already produced around four million tons of sugar, guaranteed a previously unimaginable level of national income. Those profits remained in the hands of the sugar barons and related sectors, but brought no national social advances. Euphoric over the sales, the Cuban ruling class launched a wave of speculation that was to have disastrous consequences.

As the war ended, the European beet sugar industry began to recover by 1919, and a world excess production of sugar led the United States to lift its price controls. Anticipating an increase in consumption—and, therefore, higher prices—the Cuban sugar producers stepped up production even more. The European recovery was slow, and the price rocketed to an unprecedented 22 cents a pound. The speculative frenzy reached levels never seen before, but then supply and demand quickly drove the price down again, plummeting and finally stabilizing at around 3 cents a pound in 1920. Because of prior commercial transactions, this was catastrophic.

To protect the Cuban banks, Menocal ordered a moratorium on payments in October 1920. When this proved insufficient, he proposed a delay, but the many banks in Cuba whose assets were in the United States brought pressure to bear against this. Once again, the Cuban government yielded, and the Torriente Laws ended the moratorium in January 1921. Abandoned to their fate, most of the Cuban banks quickly went bankrupt, while the US banks, now with no competition, stepped up their Cuban investments. Thus, the Cuban economy's dependence was increased. Sugar—Cuba's main product—clearly reflected the exhaustion of the economy.

Inevitably, the economic crisis triggered important struggles by the masses. Workers went on strike throughout Cuba. There was no national workers' organization; rather, strikes were called by specific groups of workers, although increasing attempts were made to link the various sectors. The railroad workers, sugar workers, typesetters, sailors, dock workers and tobacco workers were the most powerful groups, but they were still greatly influenced by anarchist and reformist ideas. Nevertheless, two big steps forward were taken during this era: the Socialist Group of Havana was founded in 1918, and the Workers' Federation of Havana emerged in 1920.

Approaching the end of his term, and to the detriment of his own Conservative Party, Menocal decided to support presidential hopeful Alfredo Zayas, who had broken from the Liberal Party and created the National Party, which constituted a very small minority. With Menocal's support, Zayas defeated his rival, José Miguel Gómez. In a truly Machiavellian gesture, the outgoing president asked the United States to send Enoch Crowder back to Cuba to suggest anti-corruption measures and to "supervise" Zayas, who had a very bad reputation as an administrator. Crowder arrived in January 1921, and his efforts greatly hampered Zayas's first year in office.

Zayas had no grounds to complain, however. After a long wait, he had finally achieved power. He was in charge of a country whose economy was experiencing a serious crisis, a rapidly growing nation with massive unsatisfied needs and a generation of youth no longer loyal to the *mambí* leaders and who believed that immediate, decisive measures were required to counter the evident failings of the republic.

The Zayas administration (1921-25) inherited the worst of the republic's problems. In the midst of the crisis caused by the collapse of sugar prices, stabilizing the economy would have required remodeling Cuba's relations with the United States and asserting the island's independence. But this was impossible for Zayas, even if he was so inclined. Instead, in the hope of securing a loan, the new president tolerated Crowder, who was determined to clean up the island's administration and stuck his nose into every government department, "advising," imposing decisions and even taking part in the selection of what was cynically called "the honest cabinet." Crowder also sent regular instructions to the president himself. The press unanimously condemned this interference in Cuban governmental affairs, but Zayas put up with it until he had managed to win a loan of around $48 million.

Crowder's work had little or no effect because the Zayas administration was steeped in fraud that was evident, for example, in the Tarafa Law on minor ports that benefited many US sugar companies and the supposed purchase of the Convent of Santa Clara, a typical Liberal-style fraud. All this greatly discredited the government. Then, in 1922, the United States adopted the Fordney Tariff, which raised the tariff on Cuban sugar from 1.6 to 1.76 cents a pound. Finally, after 20 years of the bucolic republic, a new generation set itself the task of ending corruption and fraud and, as it became more aware of the causes of the situation in Cuba, of ending political-economic dependence on the United States.

Thus new social movements appeared during the four years of the Zayas administration as students, intellectuals, women and workers began to organize themselves. Each of these sectors had its own program, its own perspective on the situation in Cuba. In the course of the struggle, the more capable leaders—scores of whom suddenly arose in this period—began to realize the key importance of unity, not just to push through the project of any one sector, but to achieve real sovereignty, both political and economic. At the same time, they also began to recognize the true responsibility of the United States for Cuba's problems.

The ideas of university reform that were being developed at the time in Córdoba, Argentina, had a great impact in Cuba, and the students at the University of Havana—the only university in the country—began a hard-fought struggle to improve the study plans, to get rid of incompetent professors and toadies of the regime and to take an active part in running the university. As part of this struggle, the Federation of University Students (FEU) was founded in December 1922 and this was to play a very important role in Cuba's history. Julio Antonio Mella, the main force behind FEU, became the most important Cuban leader of his era. Student debates were held, and the first National Revolutionary Congress of Students was held in October 1923. In November of that same year, the FEU initiated the José Martí Popular University in which hundreds of workers and low-paid employees were given free classes.

In March 1923, some very talented young intellectuals held what became known as the Protest of Thirteen, publicly denouncing the prevailing corruption and the Zayas administration's fraudulent purchase and subsequent faked sale of the Convent of Santa Clara. Rubén Martínez Villena, the leader of this group of intellectuals, later formed the Minority Group. Other more experienced intellectuals, led by Fernando Ortiz, founded the reformist National Renewal Board in April 1923. The same month, the first National Women's Congress was held, taking the first steps toward focusing on the problems of Cuban women.

Veterans of the wars of independence and other patriotic figures created an Association of Veterans and Patriots in 1923, whose reformist program expressed the former *mambís'* disappointments. The group organized a movement supporting an uprising to remedy the situation. Martínez Villena and other young people backed the insurrection that took place in April 1924, which proved to be a one-act farce typical of the republic. Its leader, Colonel Federico Laredo Bru, let Zayas "convince" him financially to abandon the struggle. The movement served as a good lesson for Cuban youth, however, teaching them to avoid alliances with corrupt politicians of the older generation.

The workers' movement had a greater impact through strikes that were stepped up under the Zayas administration. The experience gave the working class greater cohesion, and it was decided to create a united workers' union. After many vicissitudes, the National Workers' Confederation was created in February 1925 with thousands of members. The Communist Party of Cuba (in which Julio Antonio Mella played an important part) was founded in August 1925. Thus, during the third decade of the republic, the movements of workers, the petty bourgeoisie and patriotic intellectuals made considerable progress.

Of course, the Cuban oligarchy and the US government were alert to the dangers presented by these emerging movements and recognized the need for a new president who, unlike Zayas, would take a strong stand against the nationalist forces.

They struck on a man who had been a general in the war of 1895, a prominent Liberal already infamous for his repressive actions: Gerardo Machado y Morales. North American capital ensured Machado's selection over other Liberal candidates, and his administration, which commenced on May 20, 1925, became the most powerful dictatorship in Cuba in the first half of the 20th century.

An Absolutely Necessary Decade

Nearly 25 years after the establishment of the republic, the country's serious economic problems, the administration's defects and the exacerbation of social problems demanded that the new clique in power govern with greater efficiency. But this, of course, never happened. Cuba's population, 3.96 million by 1931, was pressing for thoroughgoing reforms. But any reforms that might challenge US investments (which in 1928 amounted to an incredible $1.5 billion) or alter Cuba's dependent status would be promptly quashed by the United States. Machado therefore promoted a new economic program within the narrow limits permitted. Trusting in his excellent relations with Washington and the small recovery registered in the sugar industry after 1923, he tried to bring about some changes in the economic sphere.

His program failed to bear fruit. A reduction in the sugarcane harvest in order to balance supply and demand simply resulted in a cut in Cuba's share of sugar sales on the world market because other producers did not reduce their production. An expensive plan of public works, including the completion of the National Capitol building; the construction of the university steps; the extension of Havana's Malecón (seawall); and, finally, the construction of the Central Highway failed to have positive results. Some success was achieved in temporarily alleviating unemployment, but the downside of this was that Machado asked US banks for even more money in loans than all his predecessors. The 1927 tariff reform, the most ambitious of his projects, failed to achieve its goals, while the increase in US tariffs on foreign products to stimulate domestic production did not affect the Trade Agreement of 1902. Because Machado's reforms did not try to alter Cuba's dependence on the United States, they did not achieve the hoped-for results, and these failures set the president against the patriotic sectors of Cuban society.

At the beginning of his presidency, Machado had had the support of the oligarchy and various political groups, leading him to promote the idea of "cooperativism." In that context, an Emergency Electoral Law was promulgated in 1925. But when the regime sought an extension of powers and Machado launched his reelection campaign, his former supporters deserted him.

The traditional politicians never managed to form a common front against the nascent dictatorship since they were interested in nothing more than displacing Machado and taking power themselves. The middle classes, especially the students, showed much more determination in their efforts to oust Machado. A University Student Directorate (DEU) was created at the University of Havana in 1927 to oppose the dictatorship's extension of powers, but it was short-lived.

Julio Antonio Mella was expelled from the university in 1925 and went on a hunger strike that mobilized a broad movement on his behalf. Fleeing into exile in Mexico, Mella became a prominent Latin American revolutionary leader and was assassinated by henchmen of the Machado regime in 1929. Strike activity increased from 1930, as did protests by students and the middle class, marking the beginning of a political struggle by the Cuban people. However, neither the oligarchy nor the masses had a coherent or united plan of action. The mass protests were not unified and carried out by the different sectors separately.

In yet another split away from Liberalism, Carlos Mendieta y Montefur founded the Nationalist Union in 1929. In 1930, university students founded a new University Student Directorate, which was much stronger than its predecessor. The Student Left Wing, linked with the Communist Party, broke off from the Directorate in 1931. That same year, the pro-fascist ABC appeared on the national scene, being mainly middle-class group that was structured militarily.

The forces of the dictatorship attacked a mass meeting on September 30, 1930, killing student leader Rafael Trejo and wounding others. The university students stepped up their struggle, but the traditional political groups led by Menocal and Mendieta made a pretense of an uprising in Río Verde in August 1931 that was quickly crushed by Machado's troops. This demonstrated the old politicians' inability to lead a real process of struggle and showed the role students and workers would play later in bringing down the dictatorship.

The critical situation of the world economy after the 1929 stock market crash had extremely serious consequences for Cuba. Nothing could prevent the price of sugar from falling to between 0.71 and 0.97 cents a pound in the early 1930s. Sugar production in Cuba dropped from 5.1 million tons in 1929 to 2 million tons in 1933. Neither the Chadbourne Plan in 1930, nor the severe cutback that Cuba accepted in the International Sugar Agreement of 1931 helped to stabilize the sugar crisis. Furthermore, in 1930 the United States imposed a new tariff— the Hawley-Smoot Tariff—that raised the tariff on Cuban sugar to 2 cents a pound.

These factors, along with other economic factors, reduced Cuba's share of the sugar consumed in the United States from 52 percent in 1929 to 25 percent in 1933, and this led to a considerable increase in unemployment on the island and a great reduction in the period of the sugarcane harvest. Facing a serious economic crisis, Machado resorted to repression, thereby considerably increasing opposition to his regime.

In view of Cuba's problems, the United States decided to send a new ambassador, Benjamin Sumner Welles, to Havana in March 1933 in order to get the various sectors to come to an agreement and solve the crisis "from above." Welles's task, described as "mediation," was aimed at achieving a consensus among the political groups. Most of them—except the University Student Directorate and the Communist Party—cooperated with him. Welles failed to realize that things in Cuba had become so explosive that the class that had traditionally held political power was unable to control the situation. Moreover, Machado obstinately refused to step down until a mass strike wave forced the dictator to flee the country on August 12, 1933.

In order to maintain a Machado-style administration without Machado, Carlos Manuel de Céspedes, a colorless politician with a prestigious family name, was named provisional president. But taking advantage of a plot by the sergeants in some military garrisons, the students and the middle class deposed Céspedes on September 4. This gave rise to a new form of government, composed of five members, called the Pentarchy. The sergeants' participation in the coup saw the first appearance of Fulgencio Batista in Cuba's history.

A system of government that was so divorced from the objective needs of that time could not last long, and the Pentarchy disappeared on September 10, followed by what became known as the One Hundred Day Administration, although in reality it lasted somewhat longer than 100 days. Ramón Grau San Martín, a university professor, headed that administration, which was the highest expression that the revolution of 1930 managed to achieve. Grau San Martín played an active part in the nation's political life for decades.

The dynamic force in that administration and the most important figure in that period was a radical anti-imperialist, Antonio Guiteras Holmes, who was secretary of the interior, war and the navy. Guiteras was the cabinet member with the most advanced patriotic-revolutionary views, while Grau was a lukewarm reformist; Batista, then a colonel and head of the armed forces, represented the conservatives who were intimately linked to the US embassy. This explains why, in spite of Guiteras's efforts, the administration never adopted an anti-imperialist program of radical reforms and why it was opposed by the growing forces of the oligarchic reactionaries, while at the same time it received little support from other social sectors, such as the Communist Party.

Even though it held office for only a short time, the Grau administration, pressured by the radical sector led by Guiteras, approved some measures of great national benefit. An eight-hour workday was adopted; a law was passed stating that at least 50 percent of the workers in every workplace had to be Cubans; electricity and gas prices were reduced; women were given the right to vote; and the "Cuban" Electric Company was nationalized, all of which strengthened the bourgeoisie and did not have Washington's approval.

The social crisis and political polarization was reflected in the "Battle of the National Hotel" in October 1933, when former army officers holed up in Havana's famous hotel were forced to surrender. Batista, serving as the military branch of the US embassy (which was headed by Jefferson Caffery at the time), took advantage of the crisis to unite the traditional politicians, who were worried about the course the administration was taking. Despite Guiteras's complaints about Batista to Grau, the president chose not to remove him.

It therefore came as no surprise when a counterrevolutionary coup occurred on January 15, 1934, establishing a self-styled "revolutionary" administration. The US embassy, Batista and the traditional conservative politicians put former *mambí* Colonel Carlos Mendieta in power as their puppet. This Caffery-Batista-Mendieta administration lasted until the end of 1935. This restoration of the dependent national oligarchy's political power marked the end of the ascendant stage of the revolutionary cycle. Guiteras had to go underground and, in 1934, founded a new organization called Young Cuba, which planned an insurrection. Meanwhile, the reformist political sectors backed the Cuban Revolutionary (Authentic) Party, which was led by Grau.

To indicate his support for the new situation, the US president immediately recognized the Mendieta administration, which announced a constitutional law in February that did nothing to protect the Cuban people's interests.

In May 1934, a new reciprocal trade agreement was signed which, although it reduced the tariffs on some Cuban products, forced Cuba to make tariff concessions of up to 60 percent, thus increasing its economic dependence. A team of specialists from the United States sponsored by the Foreign Policy Association made a study of the situation in Cuba and proposed some superficial changes in the economic sphere. Those proposals were published in 1935 under the title *Problems of the New Cuba*. The national sugar crisis was not resolved, and in 1934, Washington established a new system of sugar quotas, in which Cuba's share was set at just 29.4 percent of the US market—much less than what the island needed. Under this Costigan-Jones law Cuba's sugar production was stabilized at a very low level, with no real options for growth in its main—almost only—market.

Furthermore, in May 1934, Washington did Mendieta "a big favor" by doing away with the Platt Amendment, which had been in effect for more than 30 years, largely because Cuba was already so dependent on the United States it was no longer needed.

But neither the new reciprocal trade agreement nor the abrogation of the Platt Amendment kept the Cuban people from taking part in protest demonstrations and strikes when they saw that there was no hope of a real socioeconomic transformation. The diverse and disunited revolutionary groups announced a general strike for March 1935. When the strike broke out, Fulgencio Batista repressed it savagely. The members of the Authentic Party and the ABC were largely responsible for the strike's failure—both because of their political indecisiveness and because they engaged in actions against the masses, whom they feared. Some historians consider the strike to have been the last important revolutionary act of the 1930s. Others identify the assassination of Guiteras at El Morrillo in May 1935 as marking the end of the popular struggle. In any case, the revolutionary movement of the 1930s was crushed.

4
Prelude to and Beginning of the Revolution

"Yankee troops occupied our territory. The Platt Amendment was imposed on our first constitution as a humiliating clause granting the odious 'right' of foreign intervention. Our wealth passed into their hands; they falsified our history, our administration and molded our politics to the interests of the intruders. The nation was subjected to 60 years of political, economic and cultural asphyxiation."

—Second Declaration of Havana, 1962

The Struggle over the Constitution

The political parties representing the oligarchy achieved a precarious detente that made it possible to effect a regrouping of their forces. Because of the mistrust he inspired, Mendieta was forced to resign, and an election was held in January 1936, in which Miguel Mariano Gómez was elected. Gómez was the son of former President José Miguel Gómez and a typical representative of an exhausted political class that was unable to restructure a society in crisis. In May 1936, the new president assumed the difficult task of leading and guiding the Cuban nation.

Between 1936 and 1939, Batista consolidated his position as the most important figure in the army. He promoted many of his followers, gave the troops sinecures and demonstrated his leadership ability, clearly establishing himself as the indisputable head of the military. President Miguel Mariano Gómez failed to see this, and believing that he had the Cuban people's support, opposed Batista over an insignificant matter, although what was really at stake was control of the army and the nation. In December 1936, with the consent of the US embassy, Batista got the Senate to remove the president from office. Federico Laredo Bru, the vice-president, served the rest of his term.

In 1937, responding to the critical economic situation, Batista proposed the Sugar Coordination Law, but it failed to do much in the highly unstable world market. That same year, he also proclaimed an expensive three-year plan, the real purpose of which was to provide more benefits to the military sector, but this was abandoned almost immediately. Because of Cuba's political instability and the exhaustion of the sugar market, US investments in the Cuban economy began to decline and were relocated in other countries that offered greater profits.

During Laredo Bru's time in office, a serious effort was made to draw up a new constitution that would give legal expression to the main demands of the struggle against Machado.

The international situation, in which Nazi Germany became allied with Mussolini's fascist Italy opening the way for World War II, led to efforts to help the oppressed nations, such as the support for Republican Spain, in which the intellectual Pablo de la Torriente Brau played an important part. The US government—in the name of the "Good Neighbor" policy—denounced military regimes with dictatorial leanings. Batista, who always kept his ear close to the ground concerning events in Washington, tried to moderate his image as a brutal military man by separating himself from the army and making statements of a democratic nature. He expressed his support for a constitutional assembly and the measures proposed for bringing new blood into civil society.

Two of these measures were very important for Cuba's political future. In 1938, Batista legalized all parties, including the Communist Party, which reorganized itself as the Communist Revolutionary Union Party and thereby was able to take part in the constitutional process. Further, in January 1939, reflecting what was occurring in the rest of Latin America, the Workers' Confederation of Cuba was founded, closely linked to the Communist Revolutionary Union, realizing the old dream of a single national workers' organization.

Eighty-one delegates were elected to the Constitutional Assembly, which was inaugurated in February 1940. The regrouping of political forces for this important meeting led to the triumph of the opposition bloc, in which the Authentics played a key role. The progressive national forces made a serious effort to express the Cuban people's needs in the new constitution, but right-wing members of the assembly maneuvered skillfully to blunt many of the masses' demands. The delegates finally signed the new constitution on July 1, 1940.

Even though this constitution failed to include all of the demands espoused by the revolutionary process of the 1930s, it still had a progressive character that was far superior to the Constitution of 1901, and some formulations went beyond the limits of traditional Cuban bourgeois "democracy." For example, it expressed the right to free education and outlawed large landholdings, a measure that was hard to enforce but was still significant. Because many of the assembly's sessions were broadcast on the radio, people knew who was responsible for these advances and how they had been achieved. After the constitution was signed, Fulgencio Batista was elected president, and he governed from 1940 to 1944.

During his presidential term, Cuba entered World War II as a minor ally of the United States. Just as had happened in World War I, the United States used sugar as war materiel and suspended the sugar quota system. Cuba sold all its sugar— which rose from 2.8 million tons in 1939 to 4.3 million tons in 1944—to the United States in the 1942-47 period. This increase meant a prolongation of the sugarcane harvest, which, along with other factors led to a decline in the number of workers' strikes under Batista. The support given by the Communist Party to the administration, which had declared war on the fascist powers and recognized the Soviet Union, also contributed to this period of industrial peace.

A national census taken in 1943 showed that the population was almost 4.9 million, nearly a million of whom lived in

Havana and the surrounding area. The great increase in the transportation links with the United States—especially by air— and Cuba's dependence on its northern neighbor resulted in the "Americanization" of Cuban society and the adoption of the way of life and customs of the US middle class. This was evident in the opening of US-style department stores in Cuba.

The masses still demanded the passage of laws that would make the Constitution of 1940 effective. But Batista turned a deaf ear because such laws would obviously undermine the interests of the Cuban oligarchy; moreover, his administration's main priority was to guarantee the production of sugar for the United States, which was immersed in the war, and Batista used whatever means were required to do this. Batista was succeeded as president by Ramón Grau San Martín, the leading representative of the Cuban Revolutionary (Authentic) Party, a man with considerable experience in national politics.

The Authentic Party in Power

The Authentic Party was in power for two consecutive terms: from 1944 to 1948 with President Ramón Grau San Martín and from 1948 to 1952 with President Carlos Prío Socarrás. No other party in the history of the republic had awakened so many expectations and the masses gave it tremendous support. Believing that a "real revolution" would transform Cuban life at last, hundreds of thousands of Cubans followed the Authentic Party's program of reforms with close attention, in spite of its limitations.

Grau San Martín neither responded to the Cuban people's demands nor was he interested in doing so, and his complete rejection of other political organizations, especially the communists, led him to detest party alliances. His administration was a perfect example of a laissez-faire type of government that repressed the workers' struggles.

Grau had a lot in his favor when he assumed office. World War II was coming to an end, but the United States continued to purchase the island's entire sugar harvest, so Cuba's income remained relatively stable and its share of the US market—with Cuba supplying close to 40 percent of the sugar it needed—was higher than before the war.

Cuba became a founding member of the United Nations, where the Authentic administration demonstrated some independence, and this improved Cuba's international image. The recently established General Agreement on Tariffs and Trade limited the Grau administration's possibilities for making sweeping changes to the economy, but the signing of an exclusive agreement with the United States in 1947 stimulated some domestic agricultural production.

During the Batista administration, the communists had cooperated with the government, and some communist leaders had even been members of the cabinet. Nevertheless, Grau took advantage of the tensions that arose between Moscow and Washington with the Cold War and adopted a policy of marginalizing the members of the Communist Party, which renamed itself the People's Socialist Party in 1944.

President Grau had tried to eliminate Batista's influence in the army by removing high-ranking officers who supported Batista and replacing them with his own followers. He was only relatively successful in this, but it provided him with a bunch of military men who brutally persecuted anyone who dared to struggle for social reform. As part of this policy, the Grau administration's toadies got the fifth congress of the Workers' Confederation of Cuba in 1947 to break the communists' influence in that organization, which then became just another tool in the hands of the Authentic Party. A special Group for

Repressing Subversive Activities was also created to persecute any labor leaders who remained loyal to the original Workers' Confederation of Cuba.

During Grau's term in office, the sugar workers continued their traditional militancy in demanding payment of the sugar differential—proportional increases in the workers' wages corresponding to increases in the price of sugar. Sugar workers' leader Jesús Menéndez led this campaign but it cost him his life; he was assassinated in January 1948 by an army officer who was never punished. That same year, the United States announced a new law regulating its sugar imports. Cuba was assigned 28.6 percent of the US market, which was significantly less than what Cuba had exported in the previous five-year period and grossly inadequate for meeting Cuba's economic needs.

Before leaving office, Grau had to deal with a serious split within the Authentic Party. His failure to meet the Cuban people's demands and transform the republic led to the creation of a new political party led by Eduardo Chibás, one of Grau's closest collaborators. The Cuban People's (Orthodox) Party, founded in 1947, had a reformist program that was more radical than its predecessor, emphasizing the need to clean up public administration and reestablish republican ethics. This platform and Chibás's talent for oratory won the new party the overwhelming support of the Cuban masses, who once again hoped for social and economic reforms. By the late 1940s, the Orthodox Party was the main political force in Cuba.

Carlos Prío began his four-year presidential term in 1948. He declared his intention to implement the laws that were still pending that would complement the Constitution of 1940. He did actually promulgate some of these laws, such as one that reformed the functioning of the provinces and municipalities.

However, the Authentic Party was already discredited because of his predecessor's mismanagement. At first, Prío effected some lukewarm changes in an attempt to improve his party's image and to project himself as a serious reformer, but it soon became evident that he could not remodel the status quo in Cuba, and the gangsters got control.

President Prío announced his administration would fight corruption with a policy of "new republican directions," which included considering the recommendations made by the 1950 International Bank for Reconstruction and Development's (World Bank) *Truslow Report on Cuba*. The Agricultural and Industrial Development Bank of Cuba was also established.

But it was impossible to control corruption in Cuba, because the administration itself was embroiled in unethical alliances. Gangsters and thieves constituted a basic part of the governing team, creating a terrible state of political instability. Assassinations and the settling of accounts by different factions were commonplace in the life of the capital, and Prío and his team did nothing to change this state of affairs. Rather, Prío's ministers were the worst offenders, stealing from the treasury, and their relations with the groups of gangsters were public knowledge.

This explains the enormous popularity of Chibás, the Orthodox Party leader, who made frequent radio broadcasts denouncing the government's corruption and not hesitating to name names. After failing to prove the truth of one of his accusations, he committed suicide in August 1951, and the entire nation was overcome by grief. Chibás became a symbol of political honesty, and his young followers soon made their presence felt on the political scene.

After the Authentic Party was discredited, the Orthodox Party was the only group in the desolate panorama of Cuban politics that was strong enough to instigate radical change.

Even without its revered, charismatic leader, the Orthodox Party's political program and the tradition of Chibás-style campaigns meant it was expected to win the 1952 elections.

In reality, with its democratic-reformist program, the Orthodox Party would not have been able to transform Cuba without challenging the country's dependent status. But the US embassy was worried by its nationalist program and the readiness to sacrifice of a group of brilliant young members of the party (who were much more radical politically than the traditional members of the Orthodox Party). Meanwhile, Fulgencio Batista expected to be reelected in 1952.

Weeks before the March election, Batista started visiting the US embassy and working to unite his old military colleagues. Prío knew Batista was planning something, but he did nothing to prevent it. Batista realized the weakness of his Unitary Action Party and the poor regard most Cubans had for his presidency signaled certain electoral defeat, so he skillfully played on the Cuban oligarchy's desire for a "strong man" in power who would be pleasing to Washington and would end the chaotic situation caused by the Authentic Party. This meant taking a hard line against both the gangsters and the popular movement. The result was Batista's coup against Carlos Prío on March 10, 1952.

The deposed president did nothing to oppose the military uprising and refused to lead the struggle against his overthrow, thereby dealing a terrible blow to Cuba's timid experience since 1940 with civilian-democratic government. The Orthodox Party split; some of its members made weak protests, mouthing ineffective slogans that did nothing to change the situation. The People's Socialist Party denounced the coup, but it had very few members and was quite isolated; furthermore, harsh repressive measures prevented it from leading the opposition to Batista. The Federation of University Students tried to defend the constitution, but it could do nothing more than protest energetically against the coup.

The young members of the Orthodox Party were overwhelmed by indignation and a fierce desire to fight. They realized that a radical transformation of Cuba required a break with the methods of traditional politics, ending all forms of dependence on the United States and using "new methods"—as José Martí had argued—in the struggle. The idea of an armed insurrection, which Antonio Guiteras had espoused, against the new dictatorship gained currency as the best way to bring about the real, effective socioeconomic development of Cuba.

The Batista Dictatorship and the Insurrectional Struggle

Thus, the alternative of armed struggle in order to overthrow Batista and promote a radical solution for the serious problems of Cuban society arose as a result of the traditional politicians' passivity in the face of the dictatorship. Fidel Castro, a practically unknown 26-year-old lawyer, initiated the popular insurrection against the dictatorship. He organized a large group of young people, nearly all of whom were unemployed or workers of humble origins, among whom Abel Santamaría was one of the most outstanding. They trained in secret and on July 26, 1953, they attacked the army garrisons in Bayamo and Santiago de Cuba, the latter being the second most important garrison in the country,.

When the attack on the Moncada garrison failed, the hundred young revolutionaries led by Fidel Castro had to withdraw. With a small group, Fidel fell back toward the Sierra Maestra mountains. More than 50 of the young rebels who had attacked the Moncada garrison were captured or surrendered and were savagely murdered by the army. Public opinion and the rapid mobilization of the press and ecclesiastical authorities saved the lives of the other young revolutionaries.

Starting on September 21, 1953, dozens of prisoners were brought to trial, many of whom had had nothing to do with the attack. Fidel Castro was sentenced to 15 years in prison; his brother Raúl was sentenced to 13 years; and the other rebels received sentences ranging from three to 10 years. Fidel Castro made public from prison his famous defense speech called *History Will Absolve Me*.[1] That document, which expressed democratic, social and nationalist goals, became the programmatic basis of a broad front against the dictatorship. The measures proposed included the expropriation of all goods and money obtained through fraud under the dictatorship and during previous corrupt administrations, an agrarian reform and the nationalization of the US monopolies that controlled Cuba's electric power and telephone system.

Batista won an electoral farce in 1954. In May the following year, confronted with a mass public campaign and in an effort to legitimize this election, Batista was forced to grant amnesty to Fidel Castro and his compañeros. Fidel Castro then organized his followers in the July 26 Movement, but the government harassed him so he was soon forced into exile in Mexico. From there, the movement issued its first *Manifesto to the People of Cuba* in August 1955. This was an even more radical document than *History Will Absolve Me*, although it was based on the same key points. The manifesto openly called for revolution and proposed an agrarian reform, a reduction in taxes, the reestablishment of labor laws, workers' and employees' sharing in company profits, the industrialization

1. Fidel Castro, "History will absolve me," in *Fidel Castro Reader*, (Ocean Press, 2007), pp 45-105.

of the country, a broad program for building housing and reducing rents, the nationalization of basic services, the development of education and culture, a reform of the judicial system and the confiscation of embezzled wealth.

Eighty-two revolutionaries determined to renew the armed struggle against the dictatorship left Tuxpan, Mexico, for Cuba on the cabin cruiser *Granma* on November 25, 1956. Frank País led an uprising in Santiago de Cuba on November 30 to divert attention from the landing, but a lack of synchronization resulted in the arrival of the *Granma* two days after the uprising had been put down. Government forces pursued the rebels, and they had to scatter after being caught in an ambush at Alegría de Pío; only a handful of them, led by Fidel Castro, managed to reach the Sierra Maestra mountains. In spite of harsh setbacks, the small band of guerrillas—with the help of campesinos and the incorporation of new combatants whom Celia Sánchez and Frank País recruited—gradually gained in strength. The revolutionaries seized the small garrison at La Plata on January 17, 1957; on May 28, the Rebel Army won an important victory in the Battle of El Uvero, and subsequently a solid base of operations was organized in the liberated areas of the Sierra Maestra mountains.

At the same time, the Revolutionary Directorate—another armed movement opposed to Batista, consisting mainly of students—made an unsuccessful attempt to execute Batista in the Presidential Palace on March 13, 1957. José Antonio Echeverría, president of the Federation of University Students and leader of the action, was among those killed. The March 13 Revolutionary Directorate subsequently created its own guerrilla front in the central part of the island, while other organizations, such as the People's Socialist Party, also joined the struggle against the military regime.

A column led by Raúl Castro established itself in the mountains in the northern part of Oriente province, expanding the Rebel Army's base of operations. Months later, a strike was called for April 9, 1958, but this failed. Soon afterwards, the dictatorship waged a military offensive in the Sierra Maestra mountains that the Rebel Army was able to resist. The rebels then took the initiative, which they maintained for the rest of the war. Two columns of guerrillas headed toward the western part of the country; Camilo Cienfuegos's column had the goal of reaching the westernmost part of the island, while the column commanded by the Argentine, Ernesto Che Guevara, headed for central Cuba. After crossing swamps and plains to avoid enemy harassment, both vanguard groups of the Rebel Army reached the middle of the island by the end of 1958.

The climax of the revolutionary war came when Che Guevara's column liberated the city of Santa Clara, capital of the central province, after derailing an armored train that Batista had hurriedly sent from Havana to halt the rebels' advance, while Fidel and Raúl Castro's forces besieged the cities of Santiago de Cuba and Guantánamo, respectively. These events drove Batista to flee the country on January 1, 1959. In collusion with the US embassy, Batista's military high command had drawn up contingency plans for preventing the triumph of the revolutionary forces, but they proved useless when Fidel Castro called a general strike that brought the country to a standstill.

5
The Revolutionary Government

"Winning the war was not the revolution. It gave us the right to make the revolution."

—Fidel Castro, 1959

"There is no other definition of socialism valid for us than that of the abolition of the exploitation of man by man."

—Ernesto Che Guevara

The Transition to Socialism

After the triumph, a revolutionary government was established, headed at first by a judge, Manuel Urrutia, with Fidel Castro acting as prime minister from February 13, 1959. In those early days of the revolution, the dictatorship's governmental apparatus and military structures were dismantled, war criminals were put on trial and measures benefiting the Cuban people were adopted. Among other changes, telephone rates were reduced, rents on houses and apartments were cut by 50 percent, the consumption of Cuban-made products was promoted and homes were built for people with low incomes.

Batista's extensive holdings and the property of his cronies were nationalized. The National Publishing House was created, using the printing presses of a nationalized daily newspaper, and it set about publishing inexpensive books. Private beaches were opened to the public, considerable resources were allocated for public health and education, and many of the old army garrisons were gradually turned into schools. As a result of these and other measures, the Cuban people's purchasing power was greatly increased in the first eight months of 1959. The good performance by the economy contributed to this; the economy grew by 10 percent in the first two years of the revolutionary government, and sugar production in 1959, 1960 and 1961 averaged 6.2 million tons a year—much more than the 5.4 million tons that the sugarcane harvests had averaged between 1950 and 1958.

The most important measure adopted in the first few months of 1959 was the Agrarian Reform Law.[1] Issued on May 17, it benefited hundreds of thousands of farm families, setting a limit of 402 hectares on the amount of land any one person could own, although the limit could be increased to 1340 hectares in areas with high yields. The former owners were compensated with government bonds—with the amount based on the property value they had declared for tax purposes prior to the expropriation. The National Institute of Agrarian Reform (INRA) was created, headed by Fidel Castro. All the large cattle ranches were nationalized by the end of November 1959; the land planted to sugarcane was not nationalized until after the 1960 sugarcane harvest.

The promulgation of the Agrarian Reform Law exposed the class contradictions within Cuban society and accelerated the growing confrontation with the US government, polarizing those in favor of the radical measures of the revolution and those who resisted them. President Urrutia and several members of his cabinet held fast to rightist positions, and they resigned in June and July. Urrutia was replaced as president by Osvaldo Dorticós. At the same time, Huber Matos instigated a treasonous rebellion in Camagüey.

Washington's policy toward Cuba quickly changed from attempts to change the course of the revolutionary measures to outright, ruthless aggression. In 1959, the Central Intelligence Agency considered for the first time a comprehensive plan of subversion against the Cuban government, which was presented to the US National Security Council in January 1960. After this, counterrevolutionary groups whose members were drawn from various Catholic associations and the traditional political parties began to proliferate.

---

1. See "First Agrarian Reform Law" in *Cuban Revolution Reader*, (Ocean Press, 2008), pp 56-62.

On October 26, 1959, in a climate of increased acts of sabotage, armed attacks launched from the United States and defections, the Cuban people began to organize themselves in armed militias. Two days later, the Revolutionary Courts that had functioned during the first few months of the year to try counterrevolutionaries were reopened, and on November 20 the *mambí* Procedural Law of 1896, which included the death penalty and confiscation of the property of those found guilty, came into effect.

This was accompanied by a strengthening of the government's control over the economy with the creation of the Central Planning Board and the Bank of Foreign Trade of Cuba in March and April 1960. More large landholdings, including those owned by the United Fruit Company, were nationalized after the sugarcane harvest. The major newspapers and the opposition television stations were also nationalized as a result of the open conflict between the employers' association and the workers who supported the revolution or because the owners had left the country.

Informal meetings with a Soviet envoy had begun secretly in mid-October 1959, and Anastas Mikoyan, deputy premier of the Soviet Union, visited Havana in February 1960 to inaugurate a Soviet exhibit that had already been shown in Mexico and the United States. At the end of his stay, the first trade agreement with Moscow was signed. Diplomatic relations between the two countries—which had been broken by Batista after his 1952 coup—were reestablished on May 8, 1960.

After this, acts of subversion backed by the Cuban bourgeoisie, large landowners and the members of other wealthy sectors were considerably stepped up with overt support from the United States. The French steamship *La Coubre*, loaded with a cargo of weapons and ammunition that the revolutionary government had purchased in Belgium, was blown up in the port of Havana on March 4, 1960. Seventy-five people were killed and more than 200 wounded in the explosion. At the same time as this terrorist act, the United States was sponsoring training camps in Central America for Cuban exiles, preparing them to invade the island. A few months later, the Catholic hierarchy and the many Falangist Spanish priests in Cuba began an anticommunist scare campaign against the revolution.

Acts of sabotage against the sugar industry and other key sectors of the economy, the creation of armed bands of counterrevolutionaries and terrorist attacks became daily occurrences; the United States set about destabilizing the revolutionary government in numerous ways, including threats to cut off Cuba's fuel supplies. Because the foreign-owned refineries refused to process the oil Cuba acquired from the Soviet Union after signing their first trade agreement, the revolutionary government nationalized those companies on June 28, 1960. In response, a few days later the United States eliminated Cuba's sugar quota hoping to destroy the country by closing off its main market. Consequently, between August 6 and October 24 of 1960, Cuba proceeded to nationalize all US interests on the island, including banks, large factories, mines, telephone and electricity companies and the railroads.

These measures were complemented on October 13 with the nationalization of other large foreign companies and the main assets of the Cuban capitalist class, which by this time was openly supporting the counterrevolution and the United States. All Cuban and foreign-owned companies with more than 25 workers were also nationalized. On October 19, the United States banned all trade with Cuba. Almost simultaneously, the revolutionary government promulgated the Urban Reform Law, under which people who rented houses and apartments could become their owners simply by paying rent for a given number of years (depending on the age of their house or apartment).

The United States also harassed Cuba in the international arena through the Organization of American States. When the OAS foreign ministers' meeting in Costa Rica passed some anti-Cuba resolutions, Cuba responded by adopting the First Declaration of Havana[2] in a mass meeting held on September 2, 1960. During this mass meeting, Fidel Castro announced diplomatic relations had been established with the People's Republic of China.

During the first few months of 1961, in an effort to administer the greatly enlarged government sector of the economy more efficiently, new ministries, institutions and enterprises were created, while others disappeared. These new bodies had the difficult task of restructuring Cuba's economy and foreign trade. While, in the past, merchandise had simply been imported from the United States, now it would have to be brought from very far away in large ships. In addition, industry had to be readapted so it could use Soviet raw materials and spare parts instead of those from the United States. In 1961, the Soviet Union became Cuba's most important trading partner, accounting for more than 45 percent of Cuba's foreign trade.

The first stage of the revolution was filled with challenges and saw a rapid radicalization of ideology; it also brought the founding of new revolutionary organizations, such as the Association of Young Rebels, the Federation of Cuban Women and the Committees for the Defense of the Revolution in 1960 and the National Association of Small Farmers in 1961. As part of this same process, the Bureau for Coordinating

---

2. See "First Declaration of Havana" in *Cuban Revolution Reader*, (Ocean Press, 2008), pp 79-80.

Revolutionary Activities was established in September 1960 to coordinate the work of the July 26 Movement, the March 13 Revolutionary Directorate and the People's Socialist Party.

Meanwhile, the conflict with the United States continued to worsen: diplomatic relations were broken off on January 3, 1961. The United States attacked Cuba using planes painted with Cuban insignia that had taken off from airstrips in Central America, bombing three Cuban airports on April 15, killing seven people and wounding around 50. During the funeral held for the victims the following day, Fidel Castro proclaimed for the first time that the revolution was a socialist revolution.[3]

Two days later, Brigade 2506—consisting mainly of former Batista military men and young men from wealthy families whom the CIA had organized and trained in Guatemala and Nicaragua—landed at Larga and Girón beaches on Cochinos Bay (the Bay of Pigs). The invaders were defeated by the people's militias and the Rebel Army in less than 72 hours. The Bay of Pigs defeat destroyed the counterrevolutionary forces within Cuba because many of its members were arrested and others left the country discouraged. Confrontations with the Catholic Church broke out again, and several hundred priests and other religious personnel, most of them foreigners, were asked to leave the country.

While these intense conflicts were taking place, a massive literacy campaign was underway. It had spectacular results: in just a few months, 707,000 people were taught how to read and write, reducing illiteracy in Cuba to only 3.9 percent of the population, the lowest illiteracy rate in Latin America. Private education was banned on June 6, 1961, and all private schools— both religious and lay—were nationalized.

---

3. See *Fidel Castro Reader*, (Ocean Press, 2007), pp 189-93.

Creating a Socialist State

The main characteristic of the period immediately following the victory at the Bay of Pigs was the construction of a socialist government and the defense of the revolution against subversion by the United States, continual paramilitary attacks from abroad, and the effects of the economic and trade embargo, which became a total blockade in February 1962. With the complicity of all Latin American governments except Mexico, the United States expelled Cuba from the Organization of American States in January 1962, which led to Cuba's diplomatic isolation. In response to Cuba's expulsion from the OAS, a mass meeting in Havana's Revolution Plaza in February approved the Second Declaration of Havana[4] that stated: "The duty of a revolutionary is to make revolution."

The US government then drew up a plan called Operation Mongoose aimed at promoting a counterrevolutionary uprising that would provide a pretext for direct US military intervention. The large-scale acts of sabotage and terrorist actions organized by the CIA against Cuban industrial installations caused the deaths of many people and hundreds of millions of pesos' worth of damage. But Operation Mongoose was abruptly cut off by the collateral effects of the October 1962 Missile Crisis, which took the world to the brink of an atomic conflict.

That crisis—the most dangerous in the entire history of the Cold War between the United States and the Soviet Union—began on October 22, 1962, when the US intelligence services discovered that medium-range Soviet ballistic missiles had been installed in Cuba and US President John F. Kennedy demanded their immediate withdrawal. He also ordered

---

4. See "Second Declaration of Havana" in *Fidel Castro Reader*, (Ocean Press, 2007), pp 241-67.

a naval blockade of Cuba, opening the door to a nuclear conflagration. The missiles had been installed under a secret agreement between Havana and Moscow signed in August 1962 to discourage direct US military intervention in Cuba. A week after Kennedy's threats, the Soviet Union unilaterally decided to withdraw the missiles. The Cuban revolutionary government, unhappy about the fact that those negotiations were carried out behind its back, refused to allow its territory to be inspected. Thus, the crisis ended with the United States giving a verbal assurance that it would not attack Cuba militarily but caused the first coolness between Cuba and the Soviet Union.

The last counterrevolutionary organizations in Cuba were disbanded in the years following the Missile Crisis, and the groups of counterrevolutionaries (armed and financed by the United States) that had taken up arms against the revolutionary government were definitively wiped out. In that period, the United States' undeclared war against Cuba was reduced in intensity in view of the consolidation of the revolution, the broad international support for Cuba, mainly from the other socialist countries and members of the Movement of Nonaligned Countries, and the problems Washington was facing due to its war in Vietnam.

Meanwhile, the revolutionary organizations were successful in forming a united party. The July 26 Movement, the March 13 Revolutionary Directorate and the People's Socialist Party formed the Integrated Revolutionary Organizations (ORI) in May 1961. The greater organizational ability of the PSP members, combined with Cuba's growing alliance with the Soviet Union and the adoption of socialism as the goal of the revolution, led some of the veteran leaders of that party to have more influence in the ORI and in other institutions than corresponded to the contributions they had made to the triumph of the revolution.

The sectarian policy of Aníbal Escalante, organizational secretary of the ORI, aggravated this problem by assigning important administrative and political posts to former members of the People's Socialist Party. Fidel Castro demanded Escalante's resignation in March 1962 and the ORI was then restructured to wipe out sectarianism. The United Party of the Socialist Revolution of Cuba was created to replace the ORI in May 1963. The Association of Young Rebels had already become the Union of Young Communists.

The process of integrating the revolutionary organizations was not free of difficulties and misunderstandings, such as became evident among the intellectuals in mid-1961. Fidel Castro held a meeting at the National Library with artists and the leaders of cultural institutions where he urged a policy of "Within the revolution, everything; against the revolution, nothing."[5] The Union of Writers and Artists of Cuba was founded shortly afterwards, headed by the poet Nicolás Guillén.

At this point, the government controlled a large part of the national economy. All industries, the large shoe, clothing and hardware stores, and 70 percent of agriculture had been nationalized by June 1962. A second Agrarian Reform Law was promulgated in October 1963 reducing the amount of land that could be owned by any one individual to 67 hectares. The expansion of the government's control of the economy was accompanied by a decline in industrial and agricultural productivity, which combined with the effects of the blockade; massive military mobilizations; and, above all, the tremendous

---

5. Fidel Castro, "Words to Intellectuals" in *Fidel Castro Reader*, (Ocean Press, 2007), pp 213-40.

increase in the people's purchasing power, led to a scarcity of many products. To halt speculation, prices were frozen, and a rigorous system of rationing of most basic commodities was instituted in March 1962.[6]

Rationing was also the indirect result of a decision to achieve economic development by means of rapid industrialization; it was thought that Cuba's great dependence on sugar was the reason for its underdevelopment. Two things influenced the adoption of this policy of industrialization: the prevalent Latin American views at the time on development strategies and Cuba's need to attain industrial self-sufficiency quickly as a means of ensuring the survival of the revolution. To implement this policy, new government institutions were created and an ambitious development plan for the 1962-65 period was designed with the help of the Soviet Union, China and other socialist countries.

Far from producing the expected results, the development plan led to a drop in sugar production—only 3.8 million tons in 1963, which was just a little over half the amount produced in 1961—causing a significant drop in Cuba's import capacity, which had already been hard hit by its purchases of machinery and raw materials necessary for its industrial development. Industrial investments were 18 percent lower in 1964 than in the previous year. A new strategy had to be adopted in June 1963 that once again placed the emphasis on sugar production. To reinforce that trend, Cuba and the Soviet Union signed their first long-term agreement in January 1964. Effective up to 1970, this guaranteed stable prices and a growing market for Cuba's sugar.

---

6. See "Rationing Law 1015" in *Cuban Revolution Reader*, (Ocean Press, 2008), pp 138-9.

The Search for a Cuban Model of Socialism

At the same time, public debates were held on the best system of economic management for the country and there was a discussion on whether moral or material incentives were more effective to boost productivity. This polemic was initiated by Che Guevara, then minister of industry, who opposed economic accounting (or cost-profit accounting) in state enterprises. Basing themselves on the experience of the Soviet Union and other European socialist countries, some leaders of the revolutionary government proposed a system of financial self-management that would give the enterprises autonomy and depend on material incentives for increasing productivity. Guevara argued strongly against this and called for the adoption of what he called the budgetary finance system; he was very critical of the experience of Eastern Europe and the Soviet Union, which he described as trying to build socialism with "the blunted instruments of capitalism."[7]

In 1965, Che resigned as minister and devoted himself to the revolutionary struggle to assist the liberation other peoples. He was assassinated in Bolivia in October 1967. His views on political economy eventually prevailed, although many of them when applied were sometimes carried to extremes.

After 1965, however, central planning and control were abandoned, together with contempt for accounting, financial inspections and material incentives by those who wanted to do away with monetary-mercantile relations. The inevitable low productivity that was the result of those measures made it necessary to mobilize groups of voluntary workers, especially

---

7. For more on this debate, see Ernesto Che Guevara, *Critical Notes on Political Economy*, forthcoming from Ocean Press.

for exhausting agricultural labor, such as the ambitious task of planting Havana's Green Belt in 1967 and 1968 and bringing in the 1970 sugarcane harvest in which more than a million people participated.

As part of the effort to develop a Cuban model of socialism, a "revolutionary offensive" was launched in March 1968, nationalizing all kinds of small businesses—around 58,000 in all, representing 75 percent of retail trade: restaurants, bars, repair shops, handicrafts shops and street food stalls—leaving only 30 percent of agriculture and a very small part of automotive transportation in the private sector. Self-employment was virtually eliminated.

Low productivity and labor indiscipline arising from many of the egalitarian measures were not offset by the mass mobilizations of worker and student volunteers. Sometimes, other solutions had to be found. From November 1968 modern junior high schools were built in the countryside so that students combined study with agricultural work. Urban students were also mobilized for a few weeks of agricultural labor each year.

In another expression of the construction of a different model of socialism, the Vanguard Movement was created in August 1966 and, in practice, replaced the Revolutionary Central Organization of Cuban Trade Unions. Other mass organizations were revived, such as the Federation of University Students and the Union of Secondary Students, whose main activities were assumed by the Union of Young Communists.

This process was preceded by the creation of the central committee of the Communist Party of Cuba in October 1965, headed by a political bureau consisting of the historical leaders of the armed struggle against Batista. In late 1967, a small opposition group led by Aníbal Escalante—who had been sent to Eastern Europe but was then back in Cuba—was exposed within the Communist Party of Cuba. The few members of what was called the "micro-faction," most of whom were former members of the People's Socialist Party, were arrested and held for a short time at the beginning of 1968.

Meanwhile, Cuban movies, literature, the social sciences, music, ballet and art were given a big stimulus. An example of this was the inauguration of the vanguard May Salon in Havana in 1967. The University of Havana's magazine *Pensamiento Crítico* and other publications offered articles about diverse Marxist currents, including the most important ones in Western Europe at the time. An international congress on culture was held in Havana in January 1968 attended by more than 500 delegates.

This process coincided with Cuba's growing distance from some aspects of the Soviet Union's foreign policy. This reached a critical point in late 1967 and early 1968 when Cuba openly criticized the Soviet Union's weak-kneed position on the Vietnam War, which the United States was escalating, and Moscow's lack of understanding of the guerrilla movements that were having a great impact in Latin America. Thus, Cuba's search for its own model of socialism was accompanied by differences with Soviet foreign policy; moreover, in the dispute between China and the Soviet Union, Cuba argued strongly for unity.

From the early 1960s, Cuba had supported the armed revolutionary movements in Latin America. This policy had been openly proclaimed in the Declaration of Santiago de Cuba on July 26, 1964, when Cuba claimed the right to support the revolutionary movements in those countries involved in planned attacks against the revolution. In April 1967, Che's message to the peoples of the world calling for extending the revolutionary struggle and creating new Vietnams was released through *Tricontinental* magazine in Havana.[8]

In that period, Cuba's trade with the other socialist countries declined, and commerce with some Western European countries increased. Spain, for example, became Cuba's third largest trading partner in 1966. At the same time, in order to meet the nation's growing needs and financial commitments, an ambitious plan was proposed to bring in a sugarcane harvest of 10 million tons of sugar in 1970. Even though that harvest produced a record 8.5 million tons of sugar, it fell short of its goal, and this, combined with changes taking place in the international arena, such as Velasco Alvarado's election in Peru, the triumph of Allende's Popular Unity government in Chile and the end of the Vietnam War—among other factors led to a substantial change in Cuba's economic policy.

8. Ernesto Che Guevara, "Message to the Tricontinental," in *Che Guevara Reader,* (Ocean Press, 2003), pp 350-62.

6
From Institutionalization
to the Special Period

"A revolution is not a bed of roses. A revolution is a struggle to the death between the future and the past. The old order always resists to the death, and the new society fights with all its energy to survive. Either the counterrevolution destroys the revolution or the revolution destroys the counterrevolution."

—Fidel Castro, January 2, 1961

The Institutionalization of the Revolution

In the 1970s, tensions with the United States began to ease, even though threats against Cuba continued and counterrevolutionaries living in the United States planned and paid Latin American mercenaries (including Luis Posada Carriles) to blow up a Cuban passenger plane with 73 people on board in October 1976.

Cuba turned its attention to creating new institutions and promoting economic development. Ties with the Soviet Union were considerably increased to offset the effects of the ongoing US blockade of the island, and a new economic management system that promoted greater development was adopted after the 13th Workers' Congress held in November 1973.

At the same time, Cuba increased the technical assistance it had been providing to many other countries since the triumph of the revolution and sent military contingents to Ethiopia and Angola when the governments of those countries requested assistance in confronting invasions by foreign powers.

Many elements of the Soviet model of socialism were incorporated in this period, gradually abandoning the systems adopted in the latter half of the 1960s. At first, the economic recovery resulting from the new measures was helped along by a considerable increase in the price of sugar on the international market, which rose from 3.68 cents a pound in 1970 to 29.6 cents a pound in 1974. Moreover, an important agreement with the Soviet Union was signed in December 1972 that gave Cuba a moratorium on payments of interest and principal on existing loans until 1986. This moratorium was subsequently extended for a further year. The Soviet Union's share of Cuba's foreign trade rose to 60 percent during the 1980s. As a result, the Cuban economy prospered.

Central planning and a general budget were soon reestablished, and the first five-year plan (1976-80) was drawn up. Material incentives were included in the drive to increase productivity; self-employment and the buying, selling and renting of houses were authorized; and farmers' markets and handicrafts fairs were opened. From the late 1970s, and especially in the first half of the 1980s, the standard of living of the island's nearly 10 million inhabitants was raised substantially; there was practically no unemployment; everyone had a healthy, balanced diet; and 85 percent of Cuban homes had electricity, 91 percent had televisions, 50 percent had refrigerators, 59 percent had washing machines and 69 percent had fans. Moreover, machinery was introduced to do the back-breaking work of cutting sugarcane. Whereas only 2 percent of the sugarcane had been cut by machines in 1970, that figure rose to 63 percent by 1988.

This remarkable economic growth was accompanied by the widespread adoption of the Soviet model of socialism in many aspects of Cuban life. Unfortunately, this included the negative features of dogmatism and intolerance. The consequences of this were evident in the intellectual sphere between the first National Congress on Education and Culture, held in 1971, and the creation of the Ministry of Culture in 1976. These years were later described as the "gray five-year period."

The process of institutionalizing the revolution began after the first congress of the Communist Party of Cuba in December 1975. A referendum was held on February 15, 1976, in which 95.7 percent of the electors voted for a new, socialist constitution. On July 5, 1976, a new political-administrative division of the country was established and the number of provinces was increased from six to 14. For the first time since the triumph of the revolution, the election of representatives to the municipal, provincial and national levels of government took place. The institutionalization process concluded on December 2, 1976 with the inauguration of the National Assembly in which Fidel Castro was elected president of the Council of State and the Council of Ministers. He was reelected to those positions in subsequent elections up to 2008, when health problems led him to retire from active political life.

In 1977, the US blockade was eased briefly under the Carter administration, after initial steps in this direction had been made toward the end of President Gerald Ford's term in office. Ford had authorized some modifications of the blockade, such as allowing US companies' subsidiaries in third countries to trade with Cuba. In March 1977, Washington lifted its ban on travel to Cuba by US citizens of Cuban origin; in April, a fishing agreement between the two countries was signed; and, in June, Cuba and the United States agreed to open Interests Offices (unofficial diplomatic representation) in Washington and Havana.

A few years earlier, in February 1973, an agreement had been reached to prevent skyjacking, but Cuba withdrew from it after the Cubana Airlines plane was blown up off the island of Barbados. In July 1975, the United States voted in the OAS to lift some sanctions against Cuba. Cuba reestablished diplomatic relations with most of the other Latin America nations, and an important summit meeting of the Movement of Nonaligned Countries was held in Havana in 1979.

As part of the limited easing of tensions between Havana and Washington, the Cuban government freed more than 3,000 counterrevolutionary prisoners, reducing their number to a few hundred convicted terrorists. By 1987, all but a few dozen of these prisoners had been released. Nevertheless, the normalization of relations with Washington was hindered by the US government's position on human rights, Cuba's ties with the Soviet Union and the revolution's support for the Ethiopian and Angolan governments. Nor did the United States approve of Cuba's support for the Sandinista revolution in Nicaragua, Maurice Bishop's revolutionary government on the tiny island of Grenada and the guerrilla movements in El Salvador and Guatemala.

In November 1978, the Cuban government held ground-breaking talks with Cubans who had emigrated to Miami, which led to the first large-scale family visits by Cubans living in the United States.

A few years later, in April 1980, criminal elements opposed to the revolution killed one of the Cuban guards at the Peruvian embassy in Havana and forced their way in. When the Peruvian authorities gave the criminals sanctuary, the Cuban government removed its other guards, and hundreds of other people who wanted to leave Cuba crowded into the grounds of the embassy. In response, the Cuban government unilaterally granted all those who wished to leave the island permission to do so through the port of Mariel, and consequently more than 120,000 people left for Florida by boat in just a few weeks. This again damaged Cuba's relations with the United States, and it was not until four years later that Washington reestablished legal channels for Cubans to enter the United States. Between 1984 and 1990, just over 7,000 Cubans entered the United States legally while illegal departures from Cuba fell to a new low for the revolutionary period.

But after Ronald Reagan was elected president in 1980, US aggression against Cuba increased. With the end of the brief period of relative calm in US-Cuban relations, after 1981 the Cuban government was forced to devote enormous resources to defense. The Territorial Troop Militias were organized as part of a new defensive military strategy called the "war of the entire people." In spite of the stepped-up hostility, as demonstrated in large-scale US Navy maneuvers around Cuba and in terrorist attacks on Cuba's coastline, there were fewer counterrevolutionary attacks under the Republican administrations in the 1980-92 period.

Rectification

By the mid-1980s, the Cuban economy showed some worrisome symptoms. At the same time, Cuba's relations with the Soviet Union began to be complicated by perestroika advocated by Mikhail Gorbachev, the new Soviet leader. In 1987, Cuba's imports from the capitalist countries dropped by half, while economic growth registered negative figures (down 3.5 percent), something that had not occurred in more than 15 years. Moreover, the infant mortality rate increased, and unemployment reached 6 percent—the highest figure since the triumph of the revolution.

Some of the reasons for this lay in the growing deterioration in international economic conditions, the substantial drop in profits from foreign sales and the increase in the trade deficit, together with persistent demands by Cuba's creditors. In 1986, for the first time Cuba had to suspend payments on its foreign debt to more than 100 international banks. In addition, because of Gorbachev's new policy, Cuba found it impossible to obtain new credits and financing from the Soviet Union and other socialist countries, in spite of the economic commitments made to the Cuban government. These commitments were abrogated almost immediately after President Gorbachev's visit to the island in April 1989.

The proposal for responding to these problems was announced in April 1986, during the third congress of the Communist Party of Cuba. This was described as a process of "rectifying errors and negative tendencies" or "rectification." The farmers' markets were shut down, the buying and selling of homes was prohibited, self-employment was restricted and other mechanisms based on material incentives copied from the Soviet Union were done away with. Excessive recourse to material interests, bureaucracy, technocratic analysis of socioeconomic problems, corruption, wasted resources and lack of government control were criticized.

To counter these problems, voluntary work and other ideas proposed by Che in the 1960s were revived; mini-brigades of volunteers, which had originally been created in 1971 with workers from the various centers of production and services building housing, were resurrected in order to construct hospitals, child-care centers and special schools. In addition, unnecessary free services were eliminated, wages were increased for the lowest-paid sectors and hard-currency income was considerably reduced—by 40 percent in 1985 and 1986. However, in spite of these measures, the economy showed only very modest increases in 1986, 1988 and 1989 and actually decreased in 1987 and 1990.

This was the situation when one of the most serious problems the revolution ever had to confront arose: the arrest and later trial in mid-June 1989 of several high-ranking officers of the Revolutionary Armed Forces and of the Ministry of the Interior. Four of them were found guilty of corruption and drug trafficking and were sentenced to death; they were executed in July 1989. The Cuban government acted quickly and decisively in this case, not only because it was a problem involving ethics and principles, but also to prevent these links with the international drug market from exposing Cuba to the possibility of a US invasion. Only a few months later, in a similar situation, the United States invaded Panama under the pretext of fighting the traffic in drugs.

The Special Period

The disappearance of socialism in Eastern Europe (in 1989-90) and the disintegration of the Soviet Union (in 1991), along with the tightening of the US economic blockade, placed the revolution in the most difficult situation in its entire history. The sudden serious economic crisis was the result of the simultaneous loss of markets and credits and a drop in prices. Cuba's import capacity plummeted from nearly $8 billion a year to under $2 billion, while its Gross Domestic Product dropped by 40 percent.

In response to this disastrous situation, the government decided to implement a "special period" plan that had originally been drawn up for times of war. Among other things, it ensured that what few resources existed were distributed fairly. At the same time, factories, government enterprises and other centers of production and services— including some transportation routes—were shut down in order to maintain those indispensable industries and services that had previously depended on raw materials or energy from Eastern Europe. Thus, for the second time in less than 40 years Cuba had to abruptly and radically reorganize its economy.

When the socialist camp Cuba had been a part of since the 1960s suddenly disappeared, all its foreign ties—and, to a large extent, its entire economic system—had to be drastically changed to meet the challenge of preserving the social achievements of the revolution and hold out against the US blockade.

The fourth congress of the Communist Party of Cuba was held in October 1991. This congress decided to substantially transform the requisites for party membership, allowing religious believers to join; it proposed a constitutional reform that included the direct election of deputies; it ratified the single-party system; and it laid the foundations for the creation of joint ventures with foreign capital. A few months later, the 1976 Constitution was revised and the National Assembly was renewed by direct, secret vote. These elections showed that, in spite of Cuba's pressing economic problems, most of the Cuban people supported the socialist government.

Even in the worst circumstances, the Cuban government managed to preserve the revolution's key achievements. No schools or hospitals were closed, and a basic minimum of essential foodstuffs was guaranteed. Meanwhile, the vast majority of the population had to resort to a wide range of activities to augment their incomes and solve the many problems that arose with the drastic cutbacks in food, transportation, electric power and other basic services. The impact of the sudden drop in the Cuban people's standard of living also included an abrupt decline in many social services and the extension of the black market.

The United States further tightened its blockade of Cuba with the Torricelli law, passed in October 1992, which, among other punitive measures, stated that US companies in third countries would no longer be allowed to trade with Cuba, and the Helms-Burton law, which went into effect in February 1996 and authorized US courts to impose sanctions against companies in third countries that did business with Cuba.

Another consequence of the drop in Cubans' standard of living was a great increase in illegal departures; more than 30,000 people left Cuba in flimsy vessels in the summer of 1994. This uncontrolled wave of illegal departures that had historically been encouraged by the 1966 US Cuban Adjustment Act forced Washington to sign new migration agreements with Havana in 1994 and 1995, opening the doors once again to legal emigration from Cuba. In addition, the United States pledged to send anyone picked up on the high seas back to Cuba. As a result, the number of illegal departures decreased.

In the second half of 1993, the Cuban government adopted a series of measures to promote the development of tourism and the pharmaceutical industry as the main sources of foreign currency and made several other changes, some of which departed from the socialist model that had always characterized the Cuban economy.

These measures included the authorization of self-employment; the free circulation of dollars and the opening of stores selling merchandise for dollars; the transformation of two-thirds of the state's agricultural land into cooperatives (Basic Agricultural Production Units); the promulgation of a new law on investments that opened almost every economic sector in the country to foreign capital; the reopening of farmers' markets and markets selling handicrafts and industrial products (with prices governed by supply and demand); and the legalization of individuals renting rooms to foreign visitors. These measures were aimed not only at reducing the serious effects of the crisis on precarious family incomes but also at leaving the "special period" behind as quickly as possible.

This was largely successful and Cuba was able to survive its most critical crisis and gradually the economy—agriculture, industry and services—was put back on a sound footing. The Gross Domestic Product grew at an annual rate of 2.2 percent between 1994 and 1998 and by 6.2 percent in 1999, the same year in which 1.5 million tourists visited Cuba (compared to only 200,000 tourists in 1986) and the number of joint ventures operating in Cuba increased. The excess money in circulation was partially absorbed, and a relative domestic fiscal balance was achieved; the Cuban peso was revalued in relation to the US dollar, and the government's budgetary deficit was reduced to an acceptable limit.

The positive economic balance sheet made it possible to make some important improvements in the social sphere and to reactivate Cuba's solidarity with other nations. The infant mortality rate continued to drop, to under six for every 1,000 live births; thousands of Cuban doctors went to work in other Third World nations; and a Latin America School of Medicine was opened in Havana, attended by thousands of scholarship students from other Third World countries.

A gradual recovery in traditional areas of production—such as nickel and tobacco—also began to be registered from 1995, although Cuba's Achilles' heel continued to be the high cost of sugar production. This led to a decision in 2002 to shut down and dismantle more than half the sugar mills in the country so that only 54 were operational during the 2008 sugarcane harvest.

Another negative element in this situation was the combination of the dollarization of the economy and a restrictive monetary policy that led to a considerable decline in the real wages of most Cubans. This inevitably resulted in glaring inequalities, weakening the model of social equality that has always characterized Cuban socialism.

A significant increase in the extraction of crude oil and gas made it possible to generate nearly 100 percent of electricity from Cuban oil since 2003, even though Cuban oil had generated only 4 percent of the total in 1990. Housing construction, light industry and food production all increased and there was a substantial improvement in telecommunications and the mass media with the installation of new telephone services and longer television broadcasting hours, including the inauguration of some new channels, and larger runs of newspapers and magazines. In addition, unemployment was substantially reduced.

But the new growth rates and gradual increase in economic efficiency have not yet managed to fully compensate for the accumulated negative effects of the restrictions in the most critical years (1991-94) of the "special period" and the inefficient performance of the sugar sector; recent harvests have produced less than 2 million tons of sugar. Nor have they solved the problems that stem from the systematic deterioration in the terms of trade, which is mainly caused by the persistent fall in the prices of Cuba's export products and the disproportionate increase in the prices of fuel and essential foodstuffs.

The Battle of Ideas

The case of six-year-old Elián González marked an important milestone in Cuban history. It began when the boat in which he, his mother and nine other people who were trying to reach the United States illegally sank off the coast of Florida in November 1999. Everyone drowned except little Elián who was rescued and taken to Miami. Mass demonstrations and protests were held in Havana calling for Elián's return to his father in Cuba, and the case drew international media attention. On June 28, 2000, after a long period of litigation in the United States over who should have legal custody of the child, he was finally returned to his family in Cuba.

Fidel Castro headed the campaign for Elián's return, instigating a political-ideological movement called the "battle of ideas." One aspect of this campaign was an unprecedented opening in the cultural sphere, where the emphasis was placed on defending the nation's values and identity against the encroachment of neoliberal globalization from abroad.

In education, the number of schools was increased; new classrooms were built; the number of students per teacher was reduced; and a plan drawn up for universalizing education, including the possibility of studying university majors everywhere throughout the country.

More recently, under Fidel Castro's guidance, an energy revolution was launched, based on the efficient generation of electricity and its more rational use, replacing obsolete household appliances with more modern ones that consume less energy.

Meanwhile, there was not much change in US-Cuba relations. In the mid-1980s, the Cuban-American National Foundation created Radio Martí and TV Martí, which were sponsored by the US government and directed against Cuba, and in June and September 1997, CANF contracted Central American mercenaries to set off bombs in several Havana hotels and restaurants.

Toward the end of the Clinton administration, food exports to Cuba were authorized and shipments began to arrive in December 2001 after US farmers maintained pressure on President George W. Bush to respect Clinton's policy. But the Torricelli and Helms-Burton laws remained in effect, as fruits of the hostility to the Cuban revolution espoused by CANF and the conservative sectors of US society.

On May 6, 2004, US President George W. Bush announced new measures against Cuba that included harsh restrictions on family visits and on remittances of money to the island. The Cuban government replied by taking US dollars out of circulation in Cuba and replacing them with convertible Cuban pesos (CUCs).

A constitutional referendum was held in 2002, in which Cubans voted to approve socialism as a permanent system and to maintain the basic social advances that the revolution had brought.

In his closing address on December 24, 2004, to the National Assembly, President Fidel Castro stated that Cuba was emerging from the "special period" and entering a new stage in the island's history, not only as defined by its people's higher level of education and by its scientific advances in the sphere of health, but also as seen in the cooperation agreements signed with the People's Republic of China and the Bolivarian Republic of Venezuela. The Bolivarian Alternative for the Americas (ALBA) is based on Simón Bolívar's and José Martí's dreams of Latin American integration.

The following year, on December 17, 2005, Fidel Castro spoke in the Great Hall of the University of Havana encouraging Cubans to develop their political consciousness and initiated a large-scale campaign against corruption, a campaign continued even after health problems forced the historic leader of the revolution to take things a little easier. Following the July 26 ceremony in 2006, Fidel Castro had an emergency operation, and as established in the constitution he provisionally turned over his powers to Raúl Castro, first vice-president of the Council of State and the Council of Ministers.

Speaking in Camagüey on July 26, 2007, Raúl Castro said that Cuba would not renounce its search for a renewed model of socialism and that the government would continue to protect Cuban sovereignty in the face of persisting hostility from the United States.

On February 24, 2008, the National Assembly elected Raúl Castro as president of the Council of State and the Council of Ministers. Since then, several necessary measures have been taken as part of a strategy to consolidate Cuban socialism, such as allowing individual producers to use uncultivated land and the passage of a new Social Security law. Under Raúl Castro's leadership, the country has made an enormous effort to recover from the serious damage caused by Hurricanes Gustav, Ike and Paloma in 2008.

Even after the loss of support from the former socialist bloc and in spite of the harsh blockade the United States has maintained against it for over 50 years, Cuban socialism is alive and thriving, thanks to the firm and deep roots planted among the Cuban people.

Bibliography

Arboleya Cervera, Jesús. *La contrarrevolución cubana*, Havana: Editorial de Ciencias Sociales, 1997.

Armas, Ramón de; Francisco López Segrera; and Germán Sánchez Otero. *Los partidos políticos en Cuba neocolonial 1899-1952*, Havana: Editorial de Ciencias Sociales, 1985.

Buch, Luis. *Gobierno Revolucionario Cubano: génesis y primeros pasos*, Havana: Editorial de Ciencias Sociales, 1999.

Cantón, José. *Historia de Cuba. El desafío del yugo y la estrella*, Havana: Editorial SI-MAR, S.A., 1996.

Guerra Vilaboy, Sergio, and Alejo Maldonado Gallardo. *Historia de la Revolución Cubana. Síntesis y comentario*, Quito: Ediciones La Tierra, 2005.

Ibarra, Jorge. *Cuba 1898-1921. Partidos políticos y clases sociales*, Havana: Editorial de Ciencias Sociales, 1992.

Institute of History of Cuba. *Historia de Cuba*, 3 vols., Havana: Editora Política, 1994-98.

Le Riverend, Julio. *La república. Dependencia y revolución*, Havana: Instituto Cubano del Libro, 1969.

López, Francisca. *Cuba entre la reforma y la revolución. 1925-1933*, Havana: Editorial Félix Varela, 2007.

López, Francisca; Oscar Loyola; and Arnaldo Silva. *Cuba y su historia*, Havana: Editorial Gente Nueva, 2005.

Martí Study Center. *José Martí. Obras Escogidas en tres tomos*, Havana: Editorial de Ciencias Sociales, 1992.

Morales, Mario. *La frustración nacional-reformista en la Cuba republicana*, Havana: Editora Política, 1997.

Moreno Fraginals, Manuel. *El ingenio. Complejo económico-social cubano del azúcar*, 3 vols., Havana: Editorial de Ciencias Sociales, 1978.

Pérez Guzmán, Francisco; Rolando Zulueta; and Yolanda Díaz. *Guerra de Independencia 1895-1898*, Havana: Editorial de Ciencias Sociales, 1998.

Pichardo, Hortensia. *Documentos para el estudio de la historia de Cuba*, 5 vols., Havana: Editorial de Ciencias Sociales, 1969-80.

Rodríguez, Pedro Pablo. *De las dos Américas. Aproximaciones al pensamiento martiano*, Havana: Centro de Estudios Martianos, 2002.

Sorhegui, Arturo. *La Habana en el Mediterráneo americano*, Havana: Ediciones Imagen Contemporánea, 2007.

Toro, Carlos del. *La alta burguesía cubana*, Havana: Editorial de Ciencias Sociales, 2003.

Torres, Eduardo, and Oscar Loyola. *Historia de Cuba 1492-1898. Formación y liberación de la nación*, Havana: Editorial Pueblo y Educación, 2001.

Zanetti, Oscar. *Las manos en el dulce. Estado e intereses en la regulación de la industria azucarera cubana, 1926-1937*, Havana: Editorial de Ciencias Sociales, 2004.

FIDEL CASTRO READER

An outstanding new anthology of one of history's greatest orators

At last! A comprehensive selection of one of the 20th century's most influential political figures and one of history's greatest orators, Fidel Castro.

Opening with Fidel's famous courtroom defense speech following the 1953 attack on the Moncada garrison, this anthology includes more than five decades of Fidel's outstanding oratory, right up to his recent reflections on the future of the Cuban revolution "post-Fidel."

With an extensive chronology on the Cuban revolution, a comprehensive index and 24 pages of photos, this is an essential resource for scholars, researchers and general readers.

As new leaders and social forces emerge in Latin America today, this book sheds light on the continent's future as well as its past.

ISBN 978-1-920888-88-6 (paper)

Also available in Spanish ISBN 978-1-921438-01-1

CHE GUEVARA READER

Writings on Politics and Revolution

The bestselling and most comprehensive anthology of Che Guevara's writings

Recognized as one of *Time's* "icons of the 20th century," Che Guevara became a legend in his own time and has now reemerged as a symbol for a new generation of political activists. Far more than a guerrilla strategist, Che Guevara made a profound and lasting contribution to revolutionary theory and Marxist humanism as demonstrated in this perennial bestseller.

The *Che Guevara Reader* is divided into four sections: the Cuban revolutionary war (1956-59), the years in government (1959-65); Che's writings on the major international struggles of the 1960s and his vision for Latin America; and a fascinating selection of personal letters.

It includes a comprehensive chronology of Che's life, an index, and many of his classic works, such as "Socialism and Man in Cuba" and his call to create "Two, Three, Many Vietnams," as well as some previously unpublished writings.

ISBN 978-1-876175-69-6 (paper)

Also available in Spanish ISBN 978-1-876175-93-1